FRICTION FATIGUE

FRICTION FATIGUE

WHAT THE FAILURE OF ADVERTISING MEANS FOR FUTURE-FOCUSED BRANDS

PAUL DYER

LIONCREST
PUBLISHING

FRICTION FATIGUE
What the Failure of Advertising Means for Future-Focused Brands

ISBN   978-1-5445-2078-0 *Hardcover*
       978-1-5445-2077-3 *Paperback*
       978-1-5445-2076-6 *Ebook*

LINDA -
HERE'S TO THE
FRICTIONLESS FUTURE!

CONTENTS

INTRODUCTION

When people talk about brands that are defining a new era for marketing, Patagonia is often top of mind. Their purpose-driven approach, coupled with an empirical commitment to putting people and planet ahead of profits, while still making profits, is a standard bearer for young consumers, in particular. One of their most recent campaigns, *Buy Less Demand More*, debuted in late 2020 and literally called on consumers to buy fewer clothing items. The campaign explains that consumers can help protect the earth if they buy fewer products that are longer-lasting, made from recycled materials, and can serve multiple purposes. Of course, these attributes describe Patagonia's products.

Patagonia is also notoriously stingy with advertising, preferring instead to spend its marketing resources on purpose-driven programs that benefit the environment. Perhaps this is why it caught my attention when the company, which is beloved by social media power users, ran the *Buy Less Demand More* campaign as a print ad in *The New York Times* and via OOH (out-of-home) placements as well.

The ad, which was remarked on by an article in *Fast Company*, consisted of a reversible poem that can be read both top-down and bottom-up to reveal different messages.[1] After seeing the campaign, I asked our analytics team at Lippe Taylor to evaluate the social media response—expecting to see a wave of sharing and conversation about it. Somewhat surprisingly, the response to this extremely clever campaign was relatively limited. All told, the nine news articles about the campaign were shared a combined total of 881 times according to Newswhip, and people authored just 221 tweets about it. Most of this commentary came from people in the advertising industry who expressed admiration at how clever the copy was. Here's what it said:

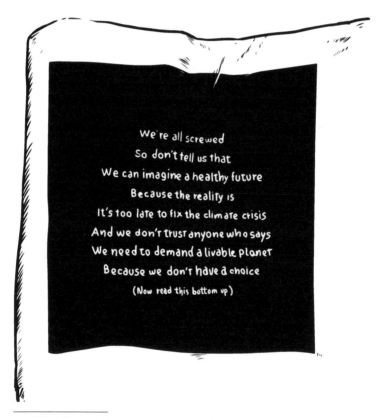

We're all screwed
So don't tell us that
We can imagine a healthy future
Because the reality is
It's too late to fix the climate crisis
And we don't trust anyone who says
We need to demand a livable planet
Because we don't have a choice
(Now read this bottom up)

1   Jeff Beer, "Patagonia's Reversible Poem Ad Is a Check on Runaway Black Friday Cyber Monday Spending," *Fast Company*, November 30, 2020, https://www.fastcompany.com/90580854/patagonias-palindrome-poem-ad-is-a-check-on-runaway-black-friday-cyber-monday-spending.

See how, when you flip the script, it's delivered in a way that even the haters have to smile at? The copy is truly a work of genius, and it was very likely produced by the advertising industry. However, the idea behind it is not an advertising idea. It's an Earned Creative idea—something that *Fast Company* naturally wrote about because it's inherently engaging.

Earlier in the year, Patagonia had a similarly Earned Creative idea that was admittedly more partisan in nature but didn't have any advertising support behind it at all. The brand printed a hidden message in its shorts during the 2020 election cycle. Flipping up the tag that was placed in the rear of the shorts revealed a hidden message that read, *Vote the Assholes Out*. Related marketing materials explained that "the assholes" were politicians who denied climate change.

Patagonia can make this call to action because it's a brand that lives its purpose. Not only does the brand donate a portion of all profits to environmental charities, but it has also designed all of its products and business practices with sustainability in mind. This commitment to living its purpose has earned Patagonia a special place in the hearts of young consumers: YPulse found that Patagonia was the number fifteen "cool" brand among millennials in 2020.[2] These consumers readily pay a premium for Patagonia's products because of the mission the company is on.

It's telling, therefore, that the brand's hidden clothing tags sparked engagement and excitement among its consumer base that was an order of magnitude greater than the response it received for its advertising campaign—despite the ad campaign being brilliant enough to garner hundreds of endorsements from advertising professionals. According to the same data sources, the hidden tags were mentioned 19,734 times. This time, the conversation centered on the message, and not everybody agreed. In fact, rather than having the ad industry talk about the clever copy, the hidden tags spawned a much more polarized conversation, which is exactly what Patagonia was going for.

Whether you agree or disagree with its message, the hidden tags are an excellent example of frictionless marketing. Rather than interrupting people, it was entirely unobtrusive, hiding there in a new pair of shorts. But it contributed to a societal conversation, aligned with a purposeful mission, and added to the customer's experience. In other words, it was everything that advertising isn't. That got me thinking: how might I borrow a page from Patagonia's book for this one? So here goes:

---

2   "Young Consumers Say These Are the 15 Coolest Clothing Brands of 2020," YPULSE, March 11, 2020, https://www.ypulse.com/article/2020/03/11/young-consumers-say-these-are-the-15-coolest-clothing-brands-of-2020/.

Advertising is merely broken
So don't tell us that
We should imagine better marketing
Because the reality is
It's not too late to fix it
And we don't trust anyone who says
It's over for Big Advertising
Because we don't have a choice
(Now read this bottom up)

Top to bottom is what the Big Advertising industrial complex would have you believe. Bottom up is closer to the truth.

The fact is, people have been foretelling the death of advertising for a long time. Despite my general disagreement with how Big Advertising conducts itself as an industry, I'm also a realist. My clients are marketers at big brands with big budgets who need to reach and influence millions of people. Until recently, it was simply not realistic to think any of the other fledgling arrows in their quiver could deliver the kind of impact they needed. So what's changed?

AMAZON GOT US HOOKED ON FRICTIONLESS

For more than two decades now, Amazon has increasingly come to define consumer expectations. They've done this largely because they have offered the consumer a better experience. In fact, "customer obsession" has been a key pillar driving Amazon's strategy from the beginning, and that customer means the consumer. In fact, the list of quotable quotes from Jeff Bezos about customer-centricity is longer than we can recount here:

"Our goal is to be earth's most customer-centric company"...."If you're

competitor-focused, you have to wait until there is a competitor doing something. Being customer-focused allows you to be more pioneering.".…"Determine what your customers need and work backward, even if it requires learning new skills.".… The list goes on, but the theme is the same.

A key pillar of Amazon's customer obsession has been **frictionless commerce**, which stems from a commonly taught microeconomics concept called frictionless markets. In frictionless markets, economists theorize about a world where transaction costs are eliminated, including things like the time required to consider and conduct a transaction as well as the actual costs to complete it. The idea is that friction caused by transaction costs decreases the volume and quality of transactions overall. By removing this friction, people will be willing to engage in more transactions. No wonder that Amazon has embraced this theory—their philosophy from the beginning has been about dominating their share of total transactions in the economy (the company famously waited fifty-eight quarters after its IPO before making a profit—all in pursuit of market dominance at all costs—even if it meant losing money).

In 1999, Amazon filed their one-click-buying patent and aggressively defended it or licensed it to others. Without the need to reenter shipping and billing information, not only did customers flow through checkout faster and abandon their carts less often, but this tech was also extended to products like Dash, which allowed one-touch reordering, Amazon Pay, which lets other websites automatically process purchases using payment information stored with Amazon, and the Echo, which allows voice ordering. Combined with two-day delivery through Prime, Amazon's frictionless shopping experience was quickly adopted by households across the country. By 2019, more than four in five American families had a Prime subscription.[3] Even in brick-and-mortar retail, recognizing the value of a frictionless in-store experience, Amazon created physical stores where customers can simply walk out (with their products in bags or backpacks) without waiting in lines, having already paid via in-store sensors and touchless payment technologies.

This idea of a frictionless commerce experience has come to define consumers' expectations overall when using their devices. Therefore, with every passing year, the deliberate interruption of advertising becomes more and more jarring in an otherwise frictionless environment.

BEING ON THE FRONT OF THE CURVE—NOT AHEAD OF IT

In an interview with *Fortune* magazine, Steve Jobs once said that "things happen fairly slowly."[4] This may seem like an un-Jobs thing to say, but he continued by explaining, "These waves of technology, you can see them way before they happen, and you just have to choose wisely which ones you're going to surf. If you choose unwisely, then you can waste a lot of energy, but if you choose wisely, it actually unfolds fairly slowly. It takes years."

The same can be said about significant changes in marketing and media. Much like with social media, digital analytics, and influencers, big trends do not happen overnight. Rather, they marinade and gain force slowly at first. Taking trends too seri-

---

3   "82 Percent of US Households Have an Amazon Prime Membership | DigitalCommerce360," https://www.digitalcommerce360. com/2019/07/11/82-of-us-households-have-a-amazon-prime-membership/.

4   "Steve Jobs Speaks Out," https://money.cnn.com/galleries/2008/fortune/0803/gallery.jobsqna. fortune/13.html.

ously when they first emerge can be a waste of resources. Waiting too long, however, can be the reason for getting left behind.

I've made my career not by being a futurist but by identifying the right time to take trends seriously. I was a recognized leader in social media marketing starting in 2007—several years after the futurists started blogging about it but at the right moment when innovative companies could create value from social media marketing. Four years later, I was on the front of the curve for digital analytics as I led the largest data science and analytics team in the industry. Then, somewhat paradoxically, I was again on the front of the curve for earned media's return to prominence in 2016.

In all of these cases, the most important theme is not being the first to predict something but having the patience and the context to determine when the right time for a trend to influence decision making occurs. IBM's Simon was the first smartphone with a touchscreen, but it was Steve Jobs's 2007 release of the iPhone that came to define the category.[5] No doubt Jobs had tracked with the technology evolutions for years, and he timed his masterpiece perfectly.

I am not the first person to foretell the death of advertising—not even close. So why, after years of futurists and disgruntled creatives alike making similar claims about the death of advertising, am I writing about it? Because even before the pandemic, which greatly accelerated these trends, a confluence of events made it clear the time has come for brand marketers to leave Big Advertising behind. I will explore each of these in greater detail throughout the book, but to give a sneak preview, five important trends gathered critical mass in the years between 2015 and 2020:

---

5   Doug Aamoth, "First Smartphone Turns 20: Fun Facts about Simon," *Time*, August 18, 2014, https://time.com/3137005/first-smartphone-ibm-simon/.

1. Consumers started migrating to ad-free and ad-light content subscriptions.
2. Michael Bloomberg provided a shockingly conclusive demonstration that advertising is no longer as effective as it once was.
3. The DTC (Direct-to-Consumer) revolution proved that brands can be built with very little advertising investment.
4. Changes in privacy policies and regulations delivered a crushing blow to Facebook's advertising platform.
5. Mass media organizations began to publicly divorce themselves from Big Advertising.

We'll look at these each briefly now and then in greater detail throughout the book.

A NOTE ON RESEARCH AND CITATIONS

I've included original and secondary research throughout this book. In some cases, the work was done by analysts at Lippe Taylor using proprietary methodologies. In addition to licensable tools like Helixa, Newswhip, and Brandwatch, our team also leverages internal technology that was developed by our own data science team. For this book in particular, we also partnered with Pollfish to execute a national consumer survey—the *Friction Fatigue Report*. Pollfish is a research partner whom we do a great deal of work with. They enable us to conduct fast consumer research at scale—often surveying hundreds or thousands of people in less than a day.

For the *Friction Fatigue Report*, we surveyed 400 people each in five different age demographics, for a total of 2,000 people overall, to understand the kind of marketing they responded to. It is a statistically representative survey in every age demographic.

In other cases, I'm simply citing research that was published in trade, business, or consumer media. This research includes annual reports like the Duke Fuqua School of Business's annual CMO survey,[6] PwC's Customer Experience Report,[7] and the Reuters Institute's Digital News Report.[8] I've made all of these resources and more, along with an explanation of various concepts from psychology and academia, available at FrictionFatigue.com.

There are also many examples and anecdotes that are provided from my personal experience and individual conversations with industry leaders. Some of these are available on the Damn Good Brands podcast,[9] where I interview C-suite leaders including chief marketing and communications officers, as well as founders, CEOs, and presidents. Wherever possible, I've done my best to credit the original source of an idea or statement.

CONSUMERS OPTED FOR SUBSCRIPTIONS OVER ADS

The cage match between consumers and advertisers, with media outlets as their octagon, dragged on for several years in the 2010s. Consumers grew increasingly irate as media outlets desperately protested the use of ad blockers. What began as Wikipedia-style appeals asking consumers to support their journalism led to media outlets deploying technology that could sniff out ad blockers. When they were detected, readers were confronted with angry messages demanding to be white-listed—as if their news site wasn't the target of the ad blockers all along. In the

---

6   Duke Fuqua School of Business's Annual CMO Survey, https://cmosurvey.org/about/cmo-insights/.

7   PwC's Customer Experience Report, https://www.pwc.com/us/en/services/consulting/library/consumer-intelligence-series.html.

8   Reuters Institute's Digital News Report, https://www.digitalnewsreport.org/.

9   Damn Good Brands podcast, https://lippetaylor.libsyn.com/.

Friction Fatigue Report, which was conducted by Lippe Taylor's analytics team in support of this book, we found that 62 percent of people with ad blockers installed would simply leave a website rather than turn off their ad blocker.

Meanwhile, behind the scenes, advertisers were pressuring media outlets to find a solution, but in the end, it was always going to end badly for advertisers. Stuck between a rock and a hard place, media outlets finally doubled down on consumers—pushing for subscription revenue in exchange for ad-free or ad-light experiences. Spotify, Netflix, and YouTube are the biggest winners to date, but plenty of other content providers, media companies, and platforms make up the long tail. Advertisers are now faced with a world where over a hundred million people have decided to pay for premium content subscriptions simply because they're sick of ads. It's hard to imagine any other product or service in history where people paid money every month to avoid having the product in their life.

MICHAEL BLOOMBERG SHATTERED THE ILLUSION OF ADVERTISING EFFECTIVENESS

The greatest campaign ever conceived by Big Advertising has been perhaps to convince marketers of its own greatness. However, it was one of their own that shattered the illusion.

In late 2019 and early 2020, Michael Bloomberg spent over $500 million on advertising in his pursuit of becoming the Democratic presidential nominee. That amount was almost $200 million more than all his other competitors combined. At any other time in history, the sheer heft of advertising spend would have at minimum guaranteed the candidate was among the front runners. Yet, Bloomberg crashed out of the race just four months after entering. For him to have spent so heavily and failed so greatly, when many considered him to be a reasonable choice, provided conclusive evidence that advertising is simply not as effective as it used to be.

DTC BRANDS PROVED YOU DON'T NEED ADVERTISING

The good news for marketers is that despite the imminent demise of their biggest weapon, plenty of evidence suggests you can still build great brands without advertising. In fact, for brands that are trying to reach millennials and Gen Z, it could be argued that an ad-light marketing mix is most effective already. According to data gathered by CircleUp, large CPG brands in the Food & Beverage category lost 19 percent of their collective market share, totaling more than $18 billion, to emerging brands between 2011 and 2015. Other categories followed suit with Beauty, Personal Care, Fashion, and Home Goods leading the charge. Overwhelmingly, these brands lacked the resources, the relationships, and the desire to follow the traditional advertising playbook.

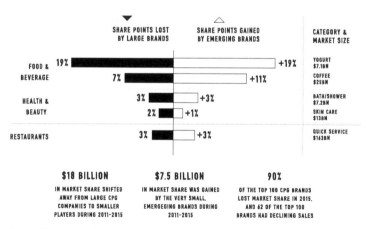

Source: Euromonitor International, Wells Fargo Securities, QSR Magazine, Statista, Boston Consulting Group, all as consolidated by CircleUp in 2018

In fact, many of the brands you think of as being massive successes with millennials and Gen Z fall into this category. Glossier, Zara, GoPro, Krispy Kreme, Sriracha, Trader Joe's, Kiehl's, and Lululemon are all examples of brands that were famously built without advertising.

Their success laid bare three important takeaways. First, that traditionally held beliefs about advertising being the only path to brand building were incomplete. Second, that entrenched brands had left themselves vulnerable by overinvesting in advertising at the expense of innovation. Third, that the consumer group with the most up-and-coming purchasing power had a preference for brands that marketed themselves differently.

FACEBOOK'S GOLDEN GOOSE GOT COOKED

It's hard to recall at this point how many scandals Facebook and its founder have endured—leading some to apply the "Teflon" label to the social network. However, the Cambridge Analytica scandal set in motion a series of events that would ultimately end with calls for reform across both sides of the aisle in Washington, DC, and a massive blow to the company's advertising platform dealt by Apple.

Until 2020, the relentless march of "performance marketing," which relied so heavily on Facebook's ad platform, seemed almost destined to dominate the marketing world. Now, with Google signaling the demise of third-party cookies and Apple's latest move allowing iPhone users to opt out of Facebook's pixel tracking, there's no doubt that Facebook's ads are going to become much less effective.

Add to this the mounting list of reasons why consumers distrust the company, including a July 2020 movement for advertisers to boycott Facebook for its refusal to monitor hate speech. Although Mark Zuckerberg was quick to diminish the impact of this movement to the company's investors, it wasn't the short-lived boycott that should have them worried. In fact, although many of the more than a thousand brands who boycotted were publicly swearing allegiance to the issue being protested, behind closed doors they admitted to being curious whether going dark with Facebook ads would have any impact on their business. The boycott provided cover for an industry-wide experiment that left many marketers realizing they could in fact decrease their use of Facebook ads for strategic reasons going forward.

MASS MEDIA DIVORCED BIG ADVERTISING

In 2017, Ev Williams, Twitter co-founder and now CEO of Medium.com, wrote, "We're trying to fight the dark forces of advertising that are destroying our minds and democracy." Williams considers his company Medium.com to be on the vanguard of journalism's war against Big Advertising. However, the war has been raging for many years, and its greatest warrior has been, without doubt, *The New York Times*.

In the year 2000, *The New York Times* made $1.3 billion or 70 percent of its revenue from advertising and 25 percent of its revenue from consumers. In 2012, those fortunes reversed with consumers accounting for the largest share of the company's much diminished revenues. By 2020, consumers accounted for fully 70 percent.

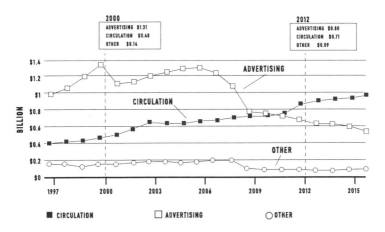

Source: New York Times Company

The path to get there was long and arduous for the iconic newspaper. In fact, it could be argued that New York University marketing professor Scott Galloway's 2008 coup saved the company. Galloway had partnered with activist hedge fund investors to raise $600 million and acquire enough shares to bully his way onto *The New York Times*' Board of Directors. The stock price by that point had dropped from the mid-$50s at the turn of the century to $17 per share, and Galloway was there to wake the company up.

He urged the company to shut off Google's free pillaging of its news content, pivot to digital over print, and double down on subscription revenue over advertising. Two years later, the stock price had further sunk to $3.50 per share, and Galloway exited the Board.

However, the seeds he planted took root, and over the next ten years, *The New York Times* became a beacon of light in the beleaguered media industry. In January 2020, a landmark report from the Reuters Institute, which studies trends in journalism, found that 50 percent of publishers believed reader revenue would be the MOST important revenue stream going forward, compared with 14 percent who said advertising would be (the balance of people said a mix of reader and advertiser revenue). In the same report the following year, subscriptions from readers were identified as the number one revenue focus going forward.

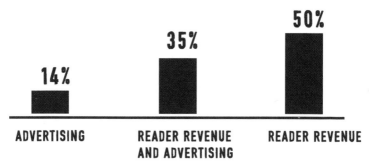

MAIN REVENUE FOCUS IN 2020
RESPONSES FROM DIGITAL LEADERS FROM 32 DIFFERENT COUNTRIES

Source: Eduardo Suárez, "How to Build a Successful Subscription News Business: Lessons from Britain and Spain," Reuters Institute, February 2020.

SUBSCRIPTION IS NOW CONSIDERED THE MOST IMPORTANT REVENUE STREAM, AHEAD OF ADVERTISING

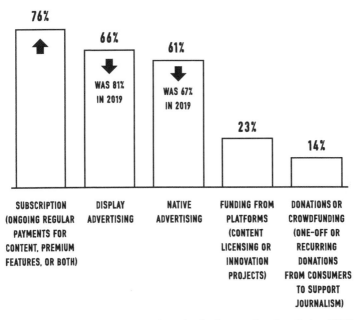

Source: Nic Newman, "Journalism, media, and technology trends and predictions 2021," Reuters Institute, January 7, 2021.

Around the same time, in corporate earnings calls across the media industry, CEOs of media conglomerates were announcing their strategic shift away from Big Advertising. As media companies start to prioritize their audiences over their advertisers, they will seek a different kind of partnership from brands. And advertising and media agencies that were accustomed to bullying both publishers and consumers alike will be forced to reckon with the realization that nobody really likes their ads.

WHY DID I WRITE THIS BOOK?

First of all, I've had the previously rare experience of being a marketer inside of PR firms, and I certainly consider myself more of a marketer rather than a publicist. I earned my MBA from the McCombs School of Business and as a consultant have spent far more time with marketing clients than PR. I've always had a foot in both worlds, though. In fact, I've been recruited by both the largest PR firm and the largest advertising agency in the world. And although these two disciplines are clearly merging, in my career I've erred on the side of PR firms because social media marketing is my true passion, and I believe the PR skillset is best suited for leading social media work.

In my time on the forefront of social media marketing, I've seen social media lead to extraordinary good in the world. Problems have been solved by remote collaboration. People have become more educated by learning from their peers. Patients with rare diseases have reached diagnoses and accessed lifesaving treatments only because social media exists. Billions of people have become more connected to friends, developed passions and hobbies, grown closer to distant relatives, and sought entertainment without being couch potatoes.

I've also seen social media do significant harm. The wave of Kardashian-inspired beauty expectations popularized by Instagram comes to mind. More seriously, social media has spurred political discourse to become more divisive than at any time since the Vietnam War. And major media outlets have become entangled on a hamster wheel of clickbait and low-brow journalism.

It's too much to blame all of these woes on advertising. But it's not an exaggeration to say that advertising and the advertising-supported content model is the single greatest force that enabled this state of affairs.

I was one of the earliest social media strategists to find a foothold, leading one Lippe Taylor interviewee to refer to me—favorably, I think—as a grandfather of social media marketing. Like most grandfathers, this perspective has given me context and perspective on how various market forces have influenced our world today.

I wrote this book as a meta-exploration of the seemingly disparate trends that are combining to wreak havoc on brand marketers at established companies and market-leading brands. It breaks down these trends along with their root causes and explains how this next generation of consumers is rewriting the rules for their relationship with marketing and media. It then offers a framework for how brand marketers can navigate the internal and external challenges facing them to find sustainable growth for their brands.

Finally, by exploring the ramifications of these trends, the challenges and pressures facing brand marketers today, and the expectations consumers have, a new framework for how to proceed will be clearer (to be discussed at length in Chapter 6). If I do my job in this book, brand marketers should go away with an updated mindset for approaching the here-and-now of marketing; but short of that, at minimum they'll gain a framework for making decisions amid the current disruption.

As a result, they might refine and optimize their existing marketing plans, or they might embrace wholesale changes in how they operate by putting the customer—that is, the ever-evolving consumer—first.

For years now, clients have relied on me to interpret data and help identify the trends that are worth acting on versus those that aren't. The truth is, although I'm a zealot for data and analytics, there is an element of gut and intuition that plays into this because in most cases, you're looking for a white space. Often, the data can tell you what *is* happening or what *isn't* happening. Sometimes it can even tell you where the proverbial puck is going. But the data will never be able to tell you if there's a different game being played down the street. That's where you need strong intuition and interpretation of trends in context. Timing is perhaps the most important aspect of intuition. Make a change too soon and you could someday be proven correct, but you will miss the window of commercial viability. The same is true of waiting too long. Timing is everything, and right now is the time to get serious about replacing advertising with a new, frictionless approach to marketing. Let's begin by looking at the state of affairs in today's media landscape and how it got to be consumerized.

THE CONSUMERIZATION OF MEDIA AND MARKETING

In 2012 and 2013, I flew from New York to LA once a month and went to Burbank to meet with the Marketing team at Warner Brothers. I was brought in by the CMO as an expert on trends in social media and how those platforms were influencing consumers. One afternoon in February 2013, I was at the Warner Brothers headquarters to speak, among other things, about a content upstart from Stockholm called Spotify.

Founded by Daniel Ek and Martin Lorentzon, Spotify began as a small startup that developed its platform in 2006 as a response to the growing piracy problem the music industry was facing. Ironically, the founder used money from the sale of his ad-tech startup in 2006 to fund his new project (he got out of advertising at the right time!). In 2008, record companies awarded Ek licensing deals they would never have struck with a US-based company. Being headquartered in Sweden meant Spotify seemed to have relatively limited potential reach.

By August 2009, while Spotify remained unavailable in the United

States, Sean Parker of Napster fame and an inspiration to Ek emailed: "Ever since Napster, I've dreamt of building a product similar to Spotify." By September, when Facebook launched its Open Graph with Spotify as a partner, the music upstart reached two million users.

The same month I visited Burbank—February 2013—Macklemore credited Spotify (and iTunes) for making "Thrift Shop" a "slow-burn hit." It seemed the company was on the cusp of something even bigger.

Far from Sweden, on the executive floor that can only be reached by a special staircase, I looked over the Warner Brothers studio lot. California sun glinted off the enormous mahogany table onto the finely pressed suit of the President of Home Entertainment, one of the company's three presidents. Filling the seats on either side of him were another dozen or so senior people, CMO included. The room was stuffy, and its inhabitants offered rare, begrudging smiles. Feeling slightly underdressed and out-manned, I reminded myself that at least I came armed with plenty of data.

I had two hours to present on trends in social media and consumer behavior, which is an incredibly long amount of time for this kind of an audience. During my talk, I told the tale of Spotify. From its quiet beginnings seven years prior as a "response to the growing piracy problem" in the music industry, Spotify had pushed their offering up an octave and turned up the volume. Arguably, they'd composed an entirely new audio landscape. What's more, listeners were not only migrating to this new territory but liked what they were hearing.

Slide after slide of data supported two important trends that seem painfully obvious today: consumers wanted to pay for content on their own terms, and they no longer got the same satisfaction from *owning* media content. Where college dorms used to be filled with display cases of CDs and DVDs, consumers today were perfectly content *renting* access to that content (now called streaming).

Although early, the trends were laid bare, in particular that streaming was going to be a big part of the future. At that time, Warner Brothers was the number one studio in the world and all eyes were on making in-home 3D movies the future of home entertainment. They had the biggest franchises in recent memory on their hands—Batman, Harry Potter, Lord of the Rings, and a dozen other blockbusters. In fact, when you look at the top ten highest grossing films ever produced by Warner Brothers, *all* of them were released between 2001 and 2014. Not only that, they had the world's largest content catalogue, worth its weight in gold.

If anyone had the opportunity to recognize these trends and do what every entertainment company is now trying to do—build streaming services—Warner Brothers did. They could have made all of their content available and cornered the market while it was still in its infancy. Late to the game but always a player, in December 2020, the company did just that. Warner Brothers Picture Group announced that *all* its 2021 films will be concurrently released for one month on streaming platform HBO Max.

Near the end of my two-hour presentation, I said, "Spotify is clearly demonstrating an important trend among consumers—that they now prefer to rent content rather than owning it."

The President of Home Entertainment raised one finger at the end of the long table (seriously, the gesture was almost cartoon-ish). It was his only interjection of the day, and the room was totally silent as everyone looked at him.

Finally, I thought, this is going to be the moment.

Instead, he replied with five words that feel as much made-in-Hollywood today as they did back then. With his entire marketing leadership team gathered around, the man with the power to corner the streaming market looked me in the eyes and said, "How do we stop this?"

By 2019, after a 19 percent year-over-year decline in sales, Warner Brothers had relinquished its place as the number one studio in the world to longtime archrival Disney and was in effect equal in size to Universal Studios. Perhaps more importantly, Netflix was occupying the nation's interest and Amazon Studios was spending a billion dollars per week on production. Meanwhile,

Spotify now has nearly 200 million global users with more than half of them paying a monthly subscription to avoid advertising.

Netflix and Spotify are leaders in the new world order in which consumers—not advertisers and not media companies—have the greatest control in this triumvirate. Consumers have taken back their power and aren't likely to relinquish it.

SPOTIFY'S AD-FREE SUBSCRIBERS 2015-2020

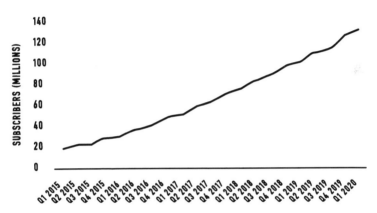

Source: "Financials," Spotify Investors, Spotify Inc.

THE TRIUMVIRATE AND THE SOCIAL CONTRACT

Since its inception, advertising has represented a social contract between marketers, media, and consumers. Marketers offered to subsidize consumers' sports, news, and entertainment experiences in exchange for them viewing ads. Media are the medium on which the transaction occurs. In this triumvirate, the consumer has always held the least power. Therefore, as tends to happen with power imbalances, the group(s) with the most power have exerted their influence over the group with the least. If we look at the latter half of the twentieth century, the golden era of the media industry, this meant that media companies exerted their power over advertisers and consumers alike.

In the 1980s, Jerry Taylor was one of the most prolific and successful publishing sales leaders in the media industry. Having been publisher of the *Lampoon* magazine, which peaked at number two on magazine racks, Jerry went on to hold roles as publisher of *Spy* magazine (famed for its sarcastic needling of prepolitical Donald Trump) and *Harper's Bazaar*. In fact, before opting to join his wife's, Maureen's, business (Lippe Taylor), Jerry declined offers to run both *Vogue* and *Playboy*.

Thinking back on the predigital media landscape, the picture Jerry paints is vastly different from today. It was a time when publishers held so much power that advertisers would shower their salespeople with gifts and incentives, vying for the opportunity to buy the best advertising slots in their publications (the first advertisement to appear when you opened the pages of *Harper's Bazaar*, for instance).

Scarcity—specifically the relative scarcity of great media content—accompanied by relatively little advertising space to reach the world's consumers, meant that media companies held all the power. This all changed with the internet but specifically with Google.

GOOGLE WAS THE HARBINGER OF CHANGE

In the early 2000s, consumers using Google, Facebook, and YouTube grew accustomed to having control over how they experienced the content they chose to consume. Perhaps the most disruptive impact, however, was Google creating the expectation that media content should be free.

Google's success in making access to information free disrupted traditional media companies more than any turmoil-inducing force that had come before it (although arguably less than Facebook has since). Until that point, most media outlets had begun adapting their existing business models to the digital era—building digital experiences that prioritized quality content but holding them behind a paywall (more on paywalls in Chapter 3). But as Google increasingly became the first point of entry for every browser session, the percentage of people who paid to access content from established media outlets plummeted.

There's a reason why Wikipedia dominates the top of Google search results—its very ethos of egalitarian, freely available information aligns perfectly with Google's mission statement. Unfortunately for the former titans of media, that mission statement is to "make the world's information universally accessible and useful." Putting content behind a paywall does not jive with this ethos, and Google punished any media outlets with paywalls accordingly by downgrading their search rank. Media outlets that sat behind a paywall all but disappeared from Google's search results.

Meanwhile, consumers shifted away from print publications to the internet. As such, the cash cow and prestige of print advertising was replaced by a digital ecosystem that demanded unimaginable amounts of content, produced rapidly and made available for free. At first, the media companies resisted, but as consumer behavior shifted and "Google it" became the primary means of finding almost anything, their capitulation became comprehensive.

Layoffs soon dominated the media landscape, and publishers were forced to survive on scraps of advertising revenue, derived from a downward spiral of selling cheap media inventory that everybody knew was wildly ineffective—banner ads. Not only do banner ad clickthrough rates hover around 0.5 percent, Inflinks proved the widespread prevalence of "banner blindness" as far back as 2013.[10] Adding insult to injury, these outlets also had to constantly adapt to Google's algorithm changes, adding costs and uncertainty on top of their decimated revenue streams.

The ensuing disruption to the media-marketer-consumer power dynamic was remarkably swift in retrospect. Media companies were on the ropes, and advertisers with their big marketing budgets held all the power. Consumers had gained access to free content, but in exchange they were about to be subjected to an increasingly overbearing onslaught of advertising.

FACEBOOK GAVE ADVERTISERS KEYS TO THE KINGDOM

Started in the mid-aughts, Facebook quickly captured the attention of millions, then billions of people. Unfortunately for consumers, Facebook did not share Google's mission-driven approach to business. Although its mission statement may claim that Facebook exists to "bring people closer together," examples abound where the company has chosen profits over people and togetherness.

This difference in philosophy played out in several important ways for advertisers and consumers.

In early 2015, a little-known big data company called Datasift was quietly aggregating something known as "topic data" inside the

---

10 "Study: 86% of Consumers Suffer from Banner Blindness," Adotas, http://www.adotas. com/2013/03/study-86-of-consumers-suffer-from-banner-blindness/.

firewall at Facebook. Datasift was the only company given this level of access, and its job was to figure out how to commercialize and sell the data through third parties. I met with the company's founder and agreed to help them use the data to develop analytics products that could be useful to marketers. We then agreed that several members of my R&D team would go on-site to explore the possibilities behind the firewall at the company's office in Reading, England. The ultimate goal as expressed by Facebook at that time was to supplant media companies as the most important advertising partner for large brands. Facebook chiefs reasoned that if advertisers were concepting creative campaigns using Facebook data, then they would naturally launch their ad campaigns on Facebook first.

Facebook did not end up launching the anonymized analytics products we designed for them. Instead, they opened up a treasure trove of information about their users to advertisers (some might call that treasure trove Pandora's box). Advertisers could now be incredibly precise, repetitive, and in fact intrusive in how they targeted consumers.

Perhaps most importantly, Facebook took advantage of pixel tracking to watch its users as they traversed the web beyond Facebook's own websites, stitching together the most comprehensive marketing dataset ever created. All of this empowered advertisers to suddenly realize the dream of targeting the "right person with the right message at the right time" to generate sales. It also drove a final stake in the heart of the traditional media outlet's sales pitch. Media companies had once claimed to have the greatest understanding of what their audiences wanted. Now Facebook was claiming to know more about their own audiences than media outlets did.

Consequently, although media companies had enjoyed power in

the previous century, and consumers had briefly glimpsed it in the early days of free internet content, Facebook had now handed advertisers the keys to the kingdom.

THE ADVERTISING INDUSTRIAL COMPLEX TAKES CONTROL, BRIEFLY

Google, Facebook, and the major media companies are only part of the Big Advertising industrial complex. Holding companies of advertising agencies and media buyers also play key roles. Paid media is how the advertising industrial complex carries out marketing services, and brand marketers compensate the publishers or platforms to feed messages to their audiences.

For the decade after the financial recession beginning in December 2007, marketers became spoiled. Consumers were cost-conscious and willing to accept a bad user experience in exchange for free content. Media companies were desperately clamoring for their ad dollars, and the new titans of industry at Google and Facebook had eliminated scarcity in advertising opportunities, while handing them a veritable cipher for reaching consumers.

Much like the preceding decade had spelled a rapid decline in power for the media outlets, the decade after the financial recession spelled a precipitous decline in power for consumers. Advertisers hungering for a competitive advantage forced consumers to fork over personally identifying information, opt into advertising-riddled commercial campaigns, and endure unending and infuriating interruptions in the form of unskippable ads, pre-roll videos, page takeovers, and retargeting campaigns that bordered on stalking. During this time, the advertising industry nearly doubled in size.

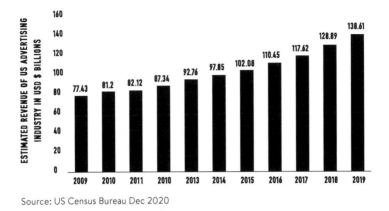

Source: US Census Bureau Dec 2020

The outcome was not good for consumers. As media outlets scraped for dollars, they continued the slow degradation of their audience's experience in order to appease the demands of their advertisers. The advertisers wanted unskippable ads. They wanted longer ads. They wanted more interruptive ads. They wanted to target people more precisely. They wanted to follow up until that person finally bought something. They wanted ads that encouraged consumers to buy right there in the ad unit. The media companies steadily gave ground, and in doing so, the consumer's experience grew worse and worse.

After Google destroyed the paywall, media companies were heavily reliant on advertising revenues to survive. *The New York Times* became the beacon of light in the industry for their ability to convince readers to pay to subscribe. But for the most part, media companies continued a slow progression toward worse and worse experiences for their audiences.

Thankfully for consumers and media outlets alike, Big Advertising's time in power was short-lived. Perhaps as a result of the breathtaking creativity they deployed in trying to force people into watching their ads, the backlash from consumers has been overwhelming.

When considering the rejection of advertising, it may seem like this change happened overnight. In fact, it happened more or less as Steve Jobs described. Twenty years of innovation gave the advertising industry plenty of time to prepare if they had heeded the warning signs. Instead, the industry seems to have been caught off guard roughly twenty years after the first obvious shots were fired across the bow.

In 1999, we got DVR from TiVo and ReplayTV. In 2002, Henrik Aasted Sørensen created the first widely used ad blocker. By 2019, GlobalWebIndex issued a report that found nearly half of all Americans were using ad blockers. The number is even higher among young people—millennials and Gen Z. In fact, a recent study titled "AdReactions" from Kantar Milward Brown found that 69 percent of Gen Z expect to be able to skip ads, whereas only 56 percent of Gen X felt the same.[11] Regardless, even using conservative math, we can estimate that more than two million ads are blocked per person every year.

---

11 "Brands Get Ready—Gen Z Are Growing Up and Ready to Challenge Says Kantar Millward Brown," https://www.prnewswire.com/news-releases/brands-get-ready---gen-z-are-growing-up-and-ready-to-challenge-says-kantar-millward-brown-610172345.html.

TOP MOTIVATIONS FOR AD-BLOCKING
% OF AD-BLOCKERS WHO REPORT THE FOLLOWING
AS THEIR MAIN REASONS FOR BLOCKING ADS

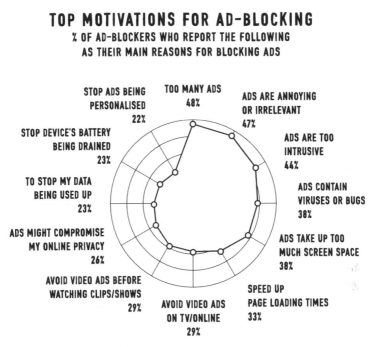

Source: Global Web Index, 2019

Without an ad blocker, the interruptions from advertising are pervasive and infuriating. Our relationship with ads has gone from ad fatigue, to ad avoidance, to ad blocking, and ultimately, to ad elimination. Premium content subscriptions have finally given consumers what I foretold the top brass at Warner Brothers all those years ago—rentable content on demand, without ads.

According to a 2016 survey of Netflix users, 90 percent would rather pay more for streaming content than watch ads, and 74 percent claim they would cancel their subscription if forced to watch ads.[12] This is not an isolated finding. Having been pushed

---

12   "74 Percent of Netflix Subscribers Would Rather Cancel Their
     Subscription than See Ads," June 21, 2016, https://blog.reelgood.
     com/74-of-netflix-subscribers-would-rather-cancel-their-subscription-than-see-ads.

to the brink by bad user experiences, consumers are past the point of ignoring or avoiding ads. They are infuriated by them.

On October 28, 2019, *The New York Times* ran an article headline, "The Advertising Industry Has a Problem: People Hate Ads."[13] In it, the article linked to a story from 2015 titled "Mad Men and the Era That Changed Advertising," which hearkened back to the 1950s. It is noteworthy because ever since Don Draper graced our television sets, there has been a palpable sense of pining for the old days in the advertising industry.

Those days are gone and good riddance. "Commercial impressions are in free fall around the world," *The New York Times* article claimed before stating that some advertisers have become so desperate they've started paying consumers to watch their ads.

WOULD YOU RATHER BE INTERRUPTED OR INTRUDED UPON?

According to a report from WARC, Facebook and Google were on track to account for nearly half of all advertising expenditure in 2019. The report didn't say half of *digital* advertising expenditure. It said half of *all* advertising expenditure.[14]

This begs the question: if consumers are rejecting advertising, how are Google and Facebook (which derive 90 percent and 98 percent of their revenue from advertising, respectively) still thriving?

---

13 Hiroko Masuike, "The Advertising Industry Has a Problem: People Hate Ads," *The New York Times*, last modified October 28, 2019, https://www.nytimes.com/2019/10/28/business/media/advertising-industry-research.html.

14 "Global Ad Trends: Global Ad Investment Forecast to Grow 6 Percent to $656 Billion in 2020," October 24, 2019, https://www.warc.com/newsandopinion/news/global_ad_trends_global_ad_investment_forecast_to_grow_6_to_656_billion_in_2020/42822.

Let's think for a minute about the traditional advertising model. The model was, by design, interruptive. Every year at the industry's boondoggle event in Cannes, advertising devotees can be witnessed practically worshipping "disruption" as a success metric.

Consumers can't be made to listen unless you "disrupt" them, and when you picture traditional advertising vehicles, they all have a familiar make and model: capture consumers' interest with sports, news, or entertainment content and then interrupt them periodically to make them view an advertisement. The same format applies to television commercials, radio and magazine ads, in-stadium scoreboards, and the headrest monitors on airplanes, among countless other examples.

Google and Facebook eschew the interruptive model by placing their ads *next to* content on their platforms instead of interrupting it and, for the most part, making the ads skippable. However, to ensure advertisers are still interested, they replaced the interruptive model with an intrusive one. Instead of offering advertisers the ability to force people to watch ads, they offer them the ability to know violatingly intimate details about people. Why bother interrupting millions of people for your condom ad when you could just target young men who recently searched for "how to have sex for the first time" instead? Why bother interrupting all the subscribers of *Cosmopolitan* with your tampon ad when you could just target the ones who recently watched a video about feminine hygiene?

This detailed understanding of consumers is what powered Google and Facebook into the juggernauts they are today. While traditional media companies were pitching advertisers in vague generalities about their viewers, tech companies were offering unprecedented details about who they were, what they liked, what they wanted, and how to influence them.

Google and Facebook loyalists would claim these companies offer consumers greater value than media companies by making the world's information searchable and helping us connect with loved ones. They would also cite both companies' contribution to democratizing the advertising industry—enabling small businesses that could never have afforded Big Advertising to promote themselves. Both of these claims are true. In late 2020, Facebook had over eight million customers placing ads through its auction model. And a reasonably compelling argument can be made for being more targeted with advertising rather than subjecting everyone to the same ads.

However, Google and Facebook also offer unprecedented power to Big Advertising, which we've seen can be wielded at the consumer's expense. In Google's case, advertisers are enabled to target people based on their **intent** (*Searching for flights to Cancun? Here's a deal to Cancun!*), while Facebook enables them to target people based on their **interests** (*I see you're a fan of cooking shows. Here's a deal for a new blender!*). Rather than needing to commit millions of dollars to "up fronts" with the media companies, advertisers can simply tune their investments up and down as they wish throughout the year.

For their part, consumers seem to have largely accepted the tradeoff. However, it's not just because Google has made information searchable or Facebook has helped them connect with friends. Both platforms have also demonstrated much greater restraint than media companies in walking the fine line of interrupting consumers.

This is of course easier to do when you have reams of data about user behavior and you can leave the expensive burden of producing content to the media companies. Nevertheless, both Google and Facebook have largely resisted the urge to introduce more interruptive ad units, opting instead to prioritize a frictionless experience for their users. With Google, this means that sponsored search results are always displayed separately from organic ones. With Facebook, this means people can easily scroll right past ads without being interrupted whether in their feeds or stories. This in itself makes the advertising experience better for the consumer.

Both companies have also pioneered "ad quality" metrics that automatically reward ads that seem to be favorably received (as measured by people clicking on them or spending more time watching their content) and punish ads that are not well received with less visibility and higher costs. This emphasis on quality extends to the advertiser overall, with advertisers who routinely run low-performing ads being punished.

Largely due to this improved value exchange in the social contract, things were going smoothly between consumers and the Google-Facebook duopoly for the better part of a decade. That is until the furor around Cambridge Analytica exploded. In the aftermath of the 2016 presidential election, media outlets revealed salacious details about a company that used Facebook ads to target individual voters with surprising precision and tune their messages in a blatant attempt to persuade them. It was exactly the same "topic data" that my engineers had accessed inside the Datasift firewall in Reading, England. However, instead of hocking advertisements for consumer products, the data was used to target voters in the election. The news cycle and accompanying outrage were deafening.

One has to assume the real fears in the Zuckerberg household during Cambridge Analytica were not actually about the political backlash but about the fact that every major marketer in America was now using Facebook ads in exactly the same way. What would happen if people were similarly outraged about being targeted by toilet paper brands as they were by political campaigns? Until 2016, the steady march toward normalization and acceptance of Facebook's Orwellian ad products seemed a foregone conclusion. However, the outrage caused by that scandal did in fact blow open the intrusiveness with which advertisers were using Facebook, leading to a domino effect of public backlash, regulation, and legislation.

CONSUMERS TAKE BACK THEIR POWER

Psychologists have a term that refers to the innately negative feelings that occur when our behavioral freedoms are limited. It's called psychological reactance. This attitudinal response describes perfectly the societal retort to Facebook, Big Advertising, and Cambridge Analytica. Writing for *Psychology Today* and citing the landmark study on reactance, psychologist Dr. Ryan Smerek explains, "Psychological reactance is the instantaneous reaction we have to being told what to do."[15]

In all cases of power imbalance and systemic manipulation, the disenfranchised party will eventually rise up. Such has been the case with consumers' rejection of Big Advertising. Whether interruptive or intrusive, the technology innovations that allowed consumers to reject advertising were years in the making. By comparison, their use of them to eliminate advertising in recent years has been swift and comprehensive. Consumers who were conditioned to expect free content from Google have evaluated

---

15   Sharon S. Brehm and Jack W. Brehm, *Psychological Reactance: A Theory of Freedom and Control* (New York: Academic Press, 1981).

the alternative advertising-supported model and decided the ads aren't worth it.

Gen Z in particular has voted with their attention, abandoning Facebook in favor of the much less intrusive and less ad-dominated TikTok and Snapchat. A July 2019 study by Business Insider found that 30 percent of Gen Z social media users "used to use Facebook but don't anymore," while Edison Research found that Facebook had dropped from being the "most commonly used" social media app for 58 percent of people age twelve to thirty-four years in 2015 to 29 percent of the same audience in 2019. Meanwhile, TikTok powered past 100 million users in the United States and closed in on one billion globally in late 2020.

WHAT SOCIAL MEDIA PLATFORMS GEN ZERS PREVIOUSLY USED BUT DON'T ANYMORE

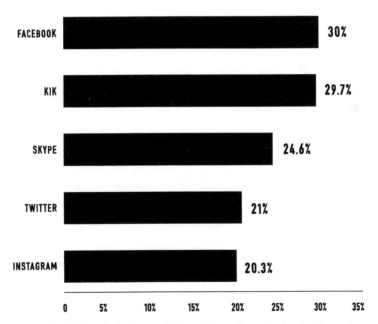

Source: Gen Z Is Abandoning Facebook, Kik, and Skype: Survey (businessinsider.com)

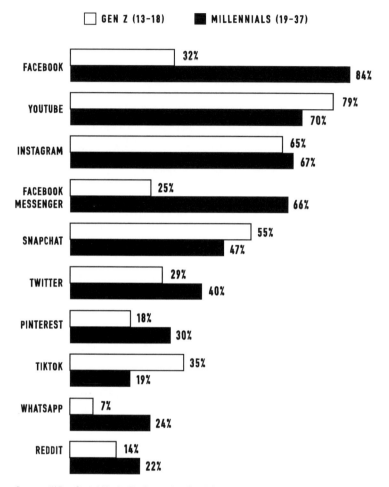

SOCIAL MEDIA PLATFORMS THEY'RE USING NOW

☐ GEN Z (13-18)   ■ MILLENNIALS (19-37)

FACEBOOK
- 32%
- 84%

YOUTUBE
- 79%
- 70%

INSTAGRAM
- 65%
- 67%

FACEBOOK MESSENGER
- 25%
- 66%

SNAPCHAT
- 55%
- 47%

TWITTER
- 29%
- 40%

PINTEREST
- 18%
- 30%

TIKTOK
- 35%
- 19%

WHATSAPP
- 7%
- 24%

REDDIT
- 14%
- 22%

Source: "What Social Media Platforms Are GenZ & Millenials Spending the Most Time on Right Now?" *YPulse*, December 14, 2020.

Despite their aversion to advertising, the takeaway is not that millennials and Gen Z dislike product or brand marketing. In fact, according to a Gartner survey in 2016, 84 percent of millennials admitted to having knowingly made a purchase after viewing user-generated content from strangers.[16] Influencers are of course the primary vehicle used by marketers to leverage this phenomenon. That same year, four in ten millennials said they trusted their favorite content creators MORE THAN their friends.[17]

By comparison, Gen Z is both more aware of and more likely to be persuaded by commercial messages from influencers. For these young consumers, it's about exerting control in the social contract. There's an implicit consent with the influencer who marketed that product because they've made a choice to follow her and have the power to unfollow her should they choose. The same thinking applies to brand social media channels, where product messages are expected and even encouraged by adoring fans, who have the choice to follow or unfollow at a moment's notice.

Even in places like Reddit, although guerilla marketers are rooted out and banned by moderators, there are accepted formats for marketing messages. Things like Ask Me Anythings (AMAs) are designed to provide a community-friendly way to promote projects, products, and ideas. Each platform and the niches within have considerations and norms, either established by the platform itself or the people who govern their feeds. Big Advertising's big mistake was to assume their historical power would allow them to continue imposing their own formats onto this new generation.

16   Chris Pemberton, "Fuel Social Marketing with User Generated Content," Gartner, https://www.gartner.com/en/marketing/insights/articles/fuel-social-marketing-user-generated-content.

17   Celie O'Neil-Hart and Howard Blumenstein, "Why YouTube Stars Are More Influential than Traditional Celebrities," Think with Google, July 2016, https://www.thinkwithgoogle.com/marketing-strategies/video/youtube-stars-influence/.

I've talked a lot about millennials and Gen Z. To dismiss the anti-advertising sentiment as being limited to young consumers would be a mistake, however. Referencing the supposed social contract between marketers, media, and consumers, what's clear is that marketers and media (or "platforms" in the cases of Google and Facebook) have trodden on the poorly defined boundaries of the social contract. Unfortunately for everyone, these guardrails were never explicitly defined. But the feeling among consumers of all ages and demographics is unanimous: marketers and media have overstepped.

The resulting disillusionment among consumers may be irreversible. We never agreed on exactly how many ads were an appropriate exchange for sports, news, and entertainment, but we can all agree that 5,000 per day is too many.[18] We never drew a red line around how intrusive advertisers could be into our lives, but the ad for that Nordstrom sweater you clicked on last fall is clearly stalking you.

This friction in digital feeds—hoisted onto increasingly fatigued consumers—reached a breaking point in the late 2010s, spawning backlash from millions of consumers who wrested control of their content experience back from advertisers, effectively consumerizing marketing.

Consumers are taking back their power by avoiding ads, installing ad blockers, and paying to eliminate ads from their content streams.

In fact, if Google and Facebook were the big winners of 2005–2015, the big winners from 2015–2020 have been Spotify and Netflix.

---

18   Sam Carr, "How Many Ads Do We See a Day in 2021?" PPC Protect, February 15, 2021, https:// ppcprotect.com/how-many-ads-do-we-see-a-day/.

Both reached multibillion-dollar market caps based on revenues collected from consumers rather than advertisers. By the start of Q4 2020, Spotify had more than 140 million worldwide premium users ("premium" users pay a monthly fee to remove ads), a 27 percent increase from a year prior and more than twice the number in 2017. Netflix has over 180 million subscribers, and CEO Reed Hastings has said the video streaming service will never drop an ad into your favorite show. That's smart, if not only because about three-quarters of the user base say they would cancel their account if Netflix did so.

SPOTIFY REVENUE AND GROSS PROFIT BY SEGMENT

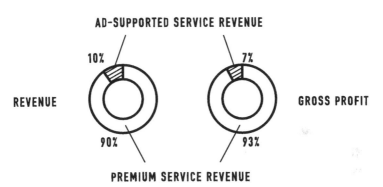

Source: Form-20, United States Securities and Exchange Commission, *Spotify Technology S.A.*, Horacio Gutierrez. Form-20, Washington, DC, December 31, 2020.

Even beyond these unique examples, the marketing case studies that stand out from the last several years all put consumers at the center. Digital "influencers" who are just regular consumers that use social media effectively have taken the industry by storm and "real people" is a phrase that has infiltrated every marketing brief. When looking at the marketing success stories from recent years, brands like Glossier and CeraVe stand out because of their direct consumer engagement (meaning the campaigns succeeded largely without significant advertising support). Even Facebook, when running its first Super Bowl ad in 2020, put consumers at the center with an ode to Facebook Groups. No matter how you look at it, the trends in marketing have been and will continue to be consumer-driven.

Of course, these trends have led to a lot of introspection within Big Advertising. But their realization has come too late, and their solutions have been to make modest adjustments to a broken model. In fact, when listening to earnings calls for advertising holding companies and keynote speeches at industry events, it's hard not to experience déjà vu. I can practically picture myself back in a stuffy conference room in Southern California where the President of Warner Brothers looked at the coming wave of streaming content and asked me, "How do we stop this?"

CHAPTER 2

ADVERTISING, AS WE KNOW IT, REALLY IS DEAD

Every year, Big Advertising flocks to the French Riviera to celebrate itself in a festival known colloquially as simply "Cannes." It's a chance for agencies to pat themselves on the back for work regardless of whether it delivered business results to clients, and its iconic awards—the Cannes Lions—have achieved almost mythical status among advertising executives. It's fitting that, set against this backdrop, Mastercard CMO and President of the World Federation of Advertisers (WFA), Raj Rajamannar, said bluntly, "Classical advertising is dead."

Advertising as we've known it is perhaps the single most frequent cause of friction in our lives. Rajamannar cites a study from Yankelovich, Inc., which claims the average person is exposed to as many as 5,000 commercial messages each day.[19] Our phones, commutes, radios, televisions, and entertainment experiences are constantly interrupted by advertising. Our local hospital has signs lining the walls proclaiming *Your Ad Here!* In fact, until very

---

19   Louise Story, "Anywhere the Eye Can See, It's Likely to See an Ad," *The New York Times*, January 15, 2007, https://www.nytimes.com/2007/01/15/business/media/15everywhere.html.

recently, advertising was as unavoidable as death and taxes. It didn't matter if you had a $10,000 television set, you were still going to see the commercials. You could buy the most expensive front-row seats to a sporting event, and your line of sight was still going to be marred with ads plastering every surface and interrupting the scoreboard display. On airplanes, it didn't matter if you were flying first class or coach; you were still going to be forced into watching commercials for the first few minutes on your headrest monitor. That all started to change with the rise of premium content subscriptions, though. NYU marketing professor and general industry curmudgeon Scott Galloway (the same Galloway who served on the Board of *The New York Times*) opined that with the rise of premium content subscriptions, "advertising is now a tax on the poor." Indeed, for the hundred million people who can afford to opt out of advertising, they have done so.

The unfortunate truth is that in order for advertising to be effective, it needs to interrupt us. The explosion of advertising has led consumers to develop an innate defense mechanism known in the industry as "advertising blindness" with some studies estimating as much as 80 percent of ads are not really "seen" as consumers gird themselves against the onslaught. In response, advertisers have become increasingly forceful in their efforts to interrupt consumers with the "disruptive" advertising being celebrated in Cannes. The result for consumers is that advertising has become a constant friction in their lives.

I had a chance to ask Rajamannar, who has overseen the rise of Mastercard's brand value from number eighty-seven to number twelve in the world, what he meant when he said advertising is dead. "People hate ads because ads are an interruption of the experience," he said. He went on to explain, "there is a narrow window which the 3,000 or 5,000 ads are trying to get through and connect with each consumer, in a context where the consumer says, 'I hate your advertisements.' So how can the situation continue?"

Marketers are not the only ones taking note of the decline of advertising. Consumers have also become aware of both the ineffectiveness and the expensiveness of advertising, leading to what can only be called an ad-shaming trend aimed at marketers who underrepresent minorities and overspend on the ads. In fact, although calls for less airbrushing, more diversity, and more realistic portrayals in advertising have perpetuated for years, 2020 was the first year that consumer outrage toward advertising extended to the opportunity cost of wasting so much money on commercials.

Set against this backdrop of purpose-driven and advertising-averse younger consumers, Budweiser, Pepsi, and Coca-Cola all announced they would NOT be buying Super Bowl commercials in 2021 with Coca-Cola fearing the optics of spending $5.5 million on thirty seconds of airtime right after laying off thousands of people, and Budweiser claiming they would be donating television commercial airtime to public service announcements for vaccine efforts. Although many applauded these decisions, social media forums also lit up with ad-shaming commentary as Anheuser Busch then ran celebrity-stuffed Super Bowl ads for four other brands besides Budweiser (overall, the company was the Super Bowl's biggest spender at over $40 million).[20]

Marc Pritchard is the Chief Brand Officer at Procter & Gamble, which is largely viewed as the most successful advertiser in the

20 Brian Steinberg, "Anheuser-Busch Pulls Budweiser From Super Bowl Ad Lineup," *Variety*, January 25, 2021, https://variety.com/2021/tv/news/super-bowl-commercials-budweiser-pulled-anheuser-busch-1234891175/.

world. Pritchard is undoubtedly the most often quoted marketing executive when it comes to topics related to advertising and brand marketing. In a 2017 speech to the American Association of Advertising Agencies, Pritchard stated, "There's too much crap...We bombard consumers with thousands of ads a day, subject them to endless load times, interrupt them with pop-ups and overpopulate their screens and feeds." Pritchard should know. According to the company's earnings report, he oversaw spending in excess of $7.2 billion worth of advertising the prior year.

Despite having correctly diagnosed the problem, however, Big Advertising's greatest patron went on to describe the solution as "focusing on fewer and better ideas that last longer." His message was that the company would focus on putting more money into media dollars and spending less on people hours, thereby demonstrating that big-brand marketers still had no idea how to live without advertising.

The combination of big advertisers spending less money on making ads worth watching and more money interrupting consumers with their low-quality ads has hastened the decline of the discipline. In 2019, ad effectiveness monitor Kantar announced—after measuring 200,000 ads—that barely a quarter of that year's Cannes Lions award-winning campaigns "provided brand impact over the short or the long-term." This was a meaningful shift. When contrasted with award-winning ads five years prior, that year's winners were "only half as effective at long-term brand building."[21]

This trend will only continue. In 2017, Forrester analyst James

21   Barry Levine, "Kantar: Award-winning ads are becoming less effective at brand building," Industry Dive, September 26, 2019, https://www.marketingdive.com/news/kantar-award-winning-ads-are-becoming-less-effective-at-brand-building/563758/.

McQuivey predicted, "It's the casual indifference to advertiser interests...that will enable consumers to finally inhabit a world free of advertising. That casual indifference is only possible because people will spend less and less of their time doing interruptible things on interruption-friendly devices."[22]

The impact of this decline in advertising effectiveness is probably most apparent when considering heritage brands (sometimes also referred to as legacy brands), which were built on the backs of advertising during the latter part of the twentieth century. These are brands many of us grew up seeing in television commercials and on the shelf in retail stores. One example of such a brand is Revlon.

In the twentieth century, Revlon was known for risk-taking and culturally relevant advertising—things like declaring in the 1950s that women wore makeup for themselves rather than to impress men, and then becoming the first major brand to feature a woman wearing pants in a television commercial for the launch of their Charlie fragrance in 1973. Charlie went on to become the number one fragrance in the world, and the risk taking continued when a subsequent print campaign caused controversy by depicting a businesswoman patting a male colleague on the backside.

By the 2010s, Revlon was still a bona fide heritage brand, but sales were slumping as millennials turned to younger, hipper brands. Anne Talley was hired as Global Brand President at Revlon to lead the turnaround with a younger generation. Speaking at Lippe Taylor's *Brand Being Summit*, Talley explained, "The disruption is happening due to the ability of startup brands to have

---

22 James L. McQuivey, "The End of Advertising, the Beginning of
    Relationships," Forrester, May 2, 2017, https://go.forrester.com/
    blogs/17-05-02-the_end_of_advertising_the_beginning_of_relationships/.

direct engagement with consumers." Revlon, like most large CPG companies, had achieved success by following a different playbook—one that prioritized retail relationships, celebrity spokesmodels, and Big Advertising.

Shortly after Anne's arrival, the company issued a well-publicized request for proposals from PR firms touting a significant investment aimed at turning the brand around. Unfortunately, as several insiders confirmed, the internal commitment to "what got them here" remained so strong that the company was unable to make real changes in how they prioritized and resourced their marketing initiatives. Nearly 90 percent of the publicized budget was spent hiring a slate of celebrities to appear in advertising, despite overwhelming evidence that competitive cosmetic brands were using a new approach. Brands like Glossier, Becca, and Fenty had focused their investments in social media, engaging directly with real consumers rather than advertising, prioritizing relatable and diverse influencers rather than celebrities, and using product collaborations as marketing efforts rather than retail shopper marketing. These brands were winning. It was a classic example of brand marketers thinking they could chart the future by using a mindset from the past.

Revlon's new Bold Brigade, as the slate of celebrities were called, did in fact represent a breakthrough for the company in the area of diverse representation in its advertising. In fact, Lippe Taylor won the RFP and played an important role in helping the company identify and publicize its most diverse cast of celebrities ever deployed. However, with the campaign relying primarily on traditional advertising to reach people, it simply reinforced entrenched perceptions among millennial consumers: Revlon really was their mother's makeup.

Let's contrast this with their father's deodorant. In one of the most famous marketing campaigns of the 2000s, Old Spice managed to turn around slumping sales with a campaign that featured a great television commercial but was largely recognized because of the digitally led consumer engagement program that followed.

OLD SPICE: THE MAN YOUR MAN COULD SMELL LIKE

Old Spice rewrote all the rules and hit a home run with this campaign, which still hails as the biggest viral marketing success of all time. On day one of the digital activation, the campaign generated more organic video views than President Obama's victory speech. Over time, more than a trillion impressions were racked up by these campaign assets. Most importantly, Old Spice body wash sales, which had declined from about 800,000 to about 650,000 units per month during the same period the previous year, now skyrocketed to nearly 1.6 million.

Michael Sabbia was the Global Brand Manager for Old Spice when *The Man Your Man Could Smell Like* burst onto the scene. Below are his words, describing how this piece of marketing history came to be:

> "This is one of those great examples of success being born out of a crisis. To paint the picture first, Old Spice was a brand that had been losing relevance for years. I mean, the word *old* was literally in our name, and Old Spice was mostly from your grandfather's generation. For that reason, your father didn't want to wear it, but now we saw an opportunity to make a comeback with this youngest generation: our original consumer's grandson.
>
> Our biggest competitor at the time was Axe, and they had really leaned into sex, but their marketing was pretty sophomoric. We knew that our 'Old' brand was never going to outsex Axe, but we had an opportunity to speak to young men as being experienced—you know, men who were wise to the world.
>
> That's when we found out that Dove for Men would be launching with a Super Bowl spot in less than three months. And that was this crisis that spurred a lot of things to happen. Much like we acknowledged that 'Old' was in our brand name, we also centered quickly on Dove's new name as an opportunity. I mean, if you have to say 'For Men' in your name (as in Dove for Men), then...well, you're not really for men. And that was where the idea of positioning against lady-scented body wash came from, with the campaign becoming *Smell Like a Man, Man*.
>
> In this case, the TV ad really was a hit. We had originally cast the main character as this white, James Bond guy, but then in walks Isaiah Mustafa with all of this panache, and he's just perfect. Thanks to that campaign, Isaiah became not just a commercial actor, but he became the Old Spice guy. So now we have a chance to engage with consumers through a real, cool, and young face of the brand.

This is when we start pushing the earned media, and you're seeing Isaiah on *Oprah* and on *Ellen DeGeneres*. Actually, the biggest turning point where the whole campaign switched from being about the advertising to being about the activation was when we got *USA Today* to run an article about Old Spice as the best commercial that DIDN'T run during the Super Bowl. It was a direct hit against Dove, who had spent millions on their Super Bowl spot, and gave us the credibility to activate the digital response campaign.

This was one of the best things about our partnership with Wieden + Kennedy. They weren't just an advertising agency for us. Every program had a digital activation and those teams were resourced as well as the ad teams. That's when we came up with the idea of having Isaiah, as the Old Spice guy, engage directly with real consumers, influencers, and celebrities over Twitter and YouTube. In less than three days, we created almost 200 videos and most of them went viral—everything from beating up a piñata for Demi Moore to helping a regular guy propose to his fiancé.

Of course, at this point, we are breaking all the rules for Procter & Gamble. Scripts were being written and videos being shot in one take. There wasn't time to schedule meetings with different teams, and there was zero legal approval for anything. Overall, the responses activation became the most viral campaign of all time, though, which I think is because we were really familiar with our audience. We were engaging with young men, age fourteen to twenty-two, and this kind of marketing was perfect for them. In fact, overall for the brand, we did a lot of things that were polarizing, and you would see the negative reactions flooding Twitter. But then you would see the positive reactions from the people we were trying to reach.

I think the other thing you have to remember is, this was not a one-hit wonder. We did a ton of digital activations on this brand, all with equal over-the-topness. And it took a lot of trust with our agency. I mean, it took a lot of trust that we're going to just go spend, because Wieden doesn't hide the fact that they spend a lot of money on these activations. And I don't know that everyone has the stomach for that kind of swinging for the fences versus hitting solid singles and doubles. But, again, that's where feeling like we were in a crisis situation actually worked to our advantage."

This inspirational and unique marketing success story is remarkable on its own, but the similarities to Revlon, which found itself in a similar position many years later, are also significant. Both were long-established heritage brands on steady declines, struggling to leverage their legacy while trying to convince new consumers they were culturally relevant today. By leaning into social media and engaging directly with consumers, Old Spice executed a historic turnaround and meteoric rise. Revlon doubled down on old-school advertising, dramatically underresourcing social media, purpose initiatives, and the things that matter to younger consumers. The company's sales peaked in 2017 and have declined every year since.

There are many factors that contribute to a brand like Revlon's fate. What's noteworthy here, however, is the failure of Big Advertising to positively impact it. Unfortunately for Big Advertising, stories like this are spreading throughout the industry, with stalwart advertisers realizing things are not what they used to be.

In June 2020, global advertising forecasts for 2021 were rather suddenly adjusted down $100 billion according to Magna. This may sound like a pandemic adjustment, but it's long overdue. For several years, spending on advertising had been incongruously rising even while consumer behavior turned against ad consumption.

Consider that in 2012 the mobile ad sales team at Yahoo! entreated major brands to buy mobile ads instead of TV ads by showing them search engine traffic during major television events, such as the Oscars. The data showed unmistakable peaks and valleys as consumers turned away from their television sets when commercials came on, using their mobile phones to search for information. Similar to Google, the positioning of Yahoo! Search ads made them much less obtrusive than television commercials. The main point, though, was that people had developed coping mechanisms to deal with the TV commercials that can be generalized as ad-avoidance behaviors.

However, despite this clear and obvious shift in consumer behavior, media buying behemoth Zenith tells us that advertising spend grew an average of 5 percent every year from 2010 through 2019, with television commercials taking the largest share.[23] How could advertising spend be rising even while consumers were tuning it out?

In many ways, the rising spend on advertising was reminiscent of how time-on-site metrics distorted website measurement reports in the early 2000s. It was assumed that longer time-on-site numbers meant visitors were happily consuming content, so designers were rewarded for increasing it as a KPI. But were tarrying visitors enjoying themselves, or were they wandering around, growing more frustrated with each click, as they struggled to find what they were looking for? Enter Amazon, which cared little how long someone was on their site; they cared if you bought what you came for, and maybe a little something extra (which didn't take long with one-click buys). In one swift stroke, the worn time-on-site wisdom was called to account. Encourag-

23 "Booming Internet Ads Power Faster Global Adspend Growth," Zenith, March 25, 2019, https://www.zenithmedia.com/booming-internet-ads-power-faster-global-adspend-growth/.

ing people to spend more time on your website when they really wanted a fast solution was bad business.

In a similar way, the rise in advertising spend during the 2010s can be largely attributed to a decline in the effectiveness of advertising. Brands needed to spend more money in order to achieve the same results they were accustomed to.

In 2020, the Democratic Party presidential primaries gave us one of the most egregious examples of the decline in advertising effectiveness, and how trying to write the future cannot be done with a mindset of the past.

CAN LIMITLESS ADVERTISING RESOURCES GUARANTEE SUCCESS?

I've thought about writing this book for many years now. The truth is, although I've always been busy, that wasn't what held me back. I delayed writing it because it wasn't the right time. So what changed for me to put pen to paper? Certainly, there are myriad convergent trends that will be discussed throughout the book. However, there was one main inspiration: Michael Bloomberg.

Former Mayor of New York City Michael Bloomberg entered the race for the Democratic Party's presidential nominee on November 19, 2019. Five days later, his campaign kicked off in Virginia with a position statement of Bloomberg as a moderate candidate with "governing experience, bravado, and financial experience," who could finally get it done versus Trump.

I first heard the news from the Lippe Taylor offices in Manhattan, and as a Political Science major and political junkie, I remember wondering, *How would this campaign be run?* His time as Mayor of New York City would be considered an asset in some house-holds and a liability in others. To illustrate the point, *The New York Times* pondered whether "issues with criminal justice and his late start" might affect his chances.[24] Many progressive voters would disdain his position in the billionaire club, but if defeating President Trump was their primary concern, he was one of the only Democrats who could draw voters from the right. In fact, he had many of the qualities that make a viable candidate in a general election.

Perhaps most importantly, it was no secret that Bloomberg had resources. If he deployed them in the right ways, he might be able to make a real run at the White House. When Bloomberg hired veteran advertising creator Bill Knapp and strategist Jimmy Seigel, it was clear the traditional playbook would be deployed. Big Advertising would lead the way with social media and grass-roots efforts playing second fiddle. For decades now, it's been widely accepted that presidential races can be swayed by simply putting more money into advertising. That's why so much atten-tion is placed on a candidate's fundraising efforts and voters are inundated with ads from every possible viewpoint.

Roughly one month into his campaign, Bloomberg had already spent $180 million across broadcast, cable, radio, and digital advertising channels. By mid-January, he said he'd be willing to spend $1 billion to beat Trump. This proclamation called to mind a particular scene in *Citizen Kane* (1941), where the protagonist Charles Foster Kane replies to an observation that his newspaper is losing money:

---

24   Alexander Burns, "Michael Bloomberg Joins 2020 Democratic Field for President," *The New York Times*, November 24, 2019, https://www.nytimes.com/2019/11/24/us/politics/michael-bloomberg-2020-presidency.html.

You're right, I did lose a million dollars last year. I expect to lose a million dollars this year. I expect to lose a million dollars *next* year. You know, Mr. Thatcher, at the rate of a million dollars a year, I'll have to close this place in...sixty years.

January campaign spending didn't disappoint, coming in at $220 million. By late February, Bloomberg's advertising outlays topped half a billion dollars. That was more than Hillary Clinton and Donald Trump spent combined in 2016...for the primary *and* the general election.

SHARE OF CANDIDATES' TV ADS
THAT RAN IN SUPER TUESDAY MEDIA MARKETS

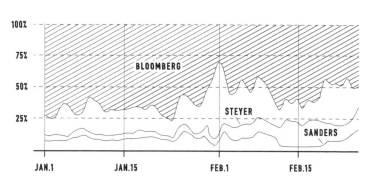

Source: Nick Corasaniti and Lazaro Gamio, "The Extraordinary Scale of Bloomberg's Ads, in 6 Charts," The New York Times, February 26, 2020.

But the advertising didn't pull its weight for Bloomberg. In fact, Bloomberg's campaign can be considered a landmark demonstration of the demise of advertising. With a mere fifty-nine delegates to his name, Bloomberg dropped out of the primary race the day after Super Tuesday. All told, he had spent about $10 million per delegate earned.

ADVERTISING WILL ALWAYS THRIVE—ONLY THE CHANNELS WILL CHANGE!

In one poll of voter intent in late February, Bloomberg soared as high as second place behind only Bernie Sanders. In January, he had spent $126.5 million on TV ads and $45.5 million on digital advertising. If only the campaign had allocated their advertising spend more wisely...That's the kind of argument I often hear from devotees of Big Advertising.

For them, advertising will always be the center of marketing; it's just that TV ads will cease to be the primary vehicle. This is a convenient position to take for entrenched advertising execs who believe they have a monopoly on creativity and persuasiveness. The argument typically goes that advertising isn't dying, only the channels are changing. To accept this argument is to miss the point entirely. Advertising is defined as:

ADVERTISING OR AD-VER-TIZ:ING [AD-VER-TAHY-ZING]

DEFINITION OF ADVERTISING

NOUN

1 THE ACT OR PRACTICE OF CALLING PUBLIC ATTENTION TO ONE'S PRODUCT, SERVICE, NEED, ETC., ESPECIALLY BY PAID ANNOUNCEMENTS IN NEWSPAPERS AND MAGAZINES, OVER RADIO OR TELEVISION, ON BILLBOARDS, ETC.

2 PAID ANNOUNCEMENTS; ADVERTISEMENTS.

3 THE PROFESSION OF PLANNING, DESIGNING, AND WRITING ADVERTISEMENTS.

Source: Dictionary.com, "Advertising," accessed April 12, 2021, https://www.dictionary.com/browse/advertising.

Unless you believe that people are generally in an "attentionless" state when confronted with an advertisement, there's no getting around that the very nature of advertising is to interrupt people.

The more money you spend, the more frequent, unavoidable, and incessant your interruption can be.

The pro-advertising camp believes these interruptions have an important role to play in our economy, that advertising will always exist, and that consumers even enjoy it. These people often allude to a now-famous quote that people don't dislike advertising—they dislike *bad* advertising. Their argument continues that even though the channels where advertising is distributed will change, advertising itself will always thrive.

This argument conflates two very different things. Marketing will always have a role to play, as will promotion. But advertising is not the same thing as marketing. As we will see in Chapter 3, advertising as it exists today is premised on a social contract between marketers, media, and consumers…and consumers are opting out of that contract en masse. Marketing will always have a role to play in society. Advertising, on the other hand, has outlived its usefulness, and the industry that built it will be dramatically reduced and reshaped over the coming decade.

YOUR ADS ARE JUST AS ANNOYING AS EVERYONE ELSE'S

In the 1980s, there was a Saint Paul, Minnesota-based radio program titled *A Prairie Home Companion*. Included in the show, which was purely fiction, was the "News from Lake Wobegon" segment. Lake Wobegon was a fictional place in which "all the children were above average," thus serving as the basis for the Lake Wobegon effect in psychology. Researchers Van Yperen and Buunk, in 1991, built on this notion by introducing a cognitive bias they named illusory superiority. Put simply, illusory superiority refers to the natural human tendency to overestimate one's own abilities. It has been proven out in any number of humorous and relatable ways—less than 1 percent of high schoolers believe themselves to be "below average" in their ability to get along with others, 80 percent of car drivers believe themselves to be "above average," and in 1987, all fifty states claimed their students tested "above the national norm."

In our *Friction Fatigue Report*, we found that across all age groups, 62.75 percent of people agree that most advertising is irritating to them. I've worked with hundreds, perhaps thousands, of marketers who make advertisements for their brands, and not one of them has believed this statistic applied to their ads. Although it's comforting to all be legends in our own minds, an overwhelming majority of advertisements are not legendary. They are irritating.

MARKETERS   AUDIENCES

Source: This image was first published on the page of VK.com user, Petersburg Punk Wall

According to Duke's annual CMO Survey, chief marketers reported their top two marketing objectives for 2021 as retaining current customers and building brand value.[25] These came ahead of raising awareness, acquiring new customers, or improving ROI. If we take them at their word, then we must assume the prevalence of interruptive advertising will plummet this year. If 62.75 percent of people believe that most ads are irritating, then only rampant illusory superiority could lead marketers to believe their ads are the exception. And if ads are irritating, then they're not building brand value or retaining your current customers.

SPONSORED MEDIA AND THE NEW PESO MODEL

For many decades there were only two forms of media—Paid and Earned. They were easily recognizable in media outlets with paid media being advertisements and earned media being editorial. There was a hard-and-fast "wall" between the two sides of the house, with entirely different teams being responsible for paid and earned media. In fact, journalists have famously resigned their posts when they felt pressures from advertising were influencing the content that went into their publications (Peter Osborne comes to mind).

With the advent of the internet and company websites, a third format gained traction called owned media. This refers to marketing assets that the marketer has complete control over—for example, their website. However, owned media has in fact existed as long as marketing has. Few people today remember, but Kraft Television Theater launched in 1947 as a way of entertaining housewives during the day. The shows were produced and "brought to you by" Kraft, which hoped the audience would remember them fondly and therefore buy the products that appeared throughout their TV show. Procter & Gamble famously

---

25   Duke's 2021 CMO Survey, https://cmosurvey.org/wp-content/uploads/2021/02/The_CMO_ Survey-Highlights_and_Insights_Report-February-2021.pdf.

expanded on the idea with what are today known as soap operas (brought to you by P&G soaps). For many people, this is still the state of things, with paid, earned, and owned media defining their opportunities to broadcast marketing messages.

However, a movement gained traction in the early 2010s to add a new media format in recognition of how social media channels offered a new, more equal playing field between marketers and their audiences. On Facebook, for example, marketers could post their messages, but so could consumers. This even playing field came to be called shared media, and the PESO (Paid, Earned, Shared, Owned) media framework picked up steam as an over-arching concept to describe the new marketing mix.

I first learned about PESO while working on-site at Red Bull, where a PESO planning matrix plotted the integrated activation of twelve-year-old skateboarding phenom Tom Schaar's attempt to land the first 1080. As a side note, this activation also illustrates the brand's commitment to investing in activations rather than just advertising. In order for Schaar to accomplish this historic feat, Red Bull had to physically reconstruct parts of the Mega Ramp at the Woodward West skate park for him. They did so even though it was entirely possible he would fail.

Source: Tom Schaar, Action, March 30, 2012, photograph, Tehachapi, California, United States, April 12, 2021.

Regardless, at this time PESO started to take off within the marketing community, and I was personally evangelizing it at every company from Procter & Gamble to Intel to Nike.

IDEA	TOM SCHAAR LANDS 1080			
	IMPACT	ENGAGEMENT	MESSAGE	CHANNEL
PAID		• FACEBOOK PAGE POST ADS • PROMOTED TWEETS • SEARCH ENGINE MARKETING ON GOOGLE & YOUTUBE TO CAPTURE INTEREST	• WORLD RECORD ATTEMPT • RED BULL HELPS TOM ACHIEVE HIS DREAM BY BUILDING RAMP EXTENSION	• FACEBOOK • TWITTER • GOOGLE • YOUTUBE
EARNED	• PR PROMOTE FEAT • BUZZ IN ACTION SPORTS BUILT TO NATIONAL		• WORLD RECORD ATTEMPT • RED BULL HELPS TOM ACHIEVE HIS DREAM BY BUILDING RAMP EXTENSION	• ENDEMIC CHANNELS: SPORTS, ACTION, NICHE • NATIONAL MEDIA
SHARED	• EMBED PLAYER ON YOUTUBE AND YAHOO SPORTS	• FACEBOOK LIKES, SHARES, COMMENTS • YAHOO/YOUTUBE VIEWS	• WORLD RECORD ATTEMPT • RED BULL HELPS TOM ACHIEVE HIS DREAM BY BUILDING RAMP EXTENSION	• YOUTUBE • YAHOO SPORTS
OWNED	• ACTION CLIP OFFERED EXCLUSIVELY ON RB PLAYER FOR 48HRS • ACTION CLIP AND STORY CLIP OFFERED ON CP AFTER 48HRS • POST VIDEO ON REDBULL.COM • EMBED PLAYER ON FACEBOOK/TWITTER LINK • FACEBOOK/TWITTER POSTS • STRATEGIC NAMING OF EVENT WITH RED BULL IN THE TITLE	• VIEWS: REDBULL.COM AND SOCIAL MEDIA PAGE TRAFFIC • NEW USERS AND ADDED TRAFFIC TO CONTENT POOL • GREATER CONNECTION WITH RED BULL	• WORLD RECORD ATTEMPT • RED BULL HELPS TOM ACHIEVE HIS DREAM BY BUILDING RAMP EXTENSION	• REDBULL.COM • FACEBOOK • TWITTER • INSTAGRAM

At that time, most people agreed the marketing formats had evolved sufficiently that more nuance was required, but many still challenged the notion of a shared media format. In their eyes, social media either was or would become defined by the three existing mediums: Paid for social ads, Earned for organic conversation, and Owned for branded content. In retrospect, they were right. That is exactly what happened.

However, in recent years a new media format has emerged that deserves much more serious consideration as part of the media mix, largely because it is also being offered as a promotion vehicle by major media outlets. The format could also be described by an *S* moniker to fit within the PESO acronym. That is to say, instead of shared media, the new PESO ought to include sponsored media.

Sponsored media refers to a variety of efforts in which a third party is promoting a marketing message with a level of independence, but the marketer pays to exert a degree of control over the final content. Perhaps the most obvious example today is influencer marketing, where marketers pay digital influencers a fee and the influencers sign a contract stating they will adhere to certain brand guidelines. The influencers then create content as they see fit, with the brand having certain approval rights. This type of promotion is neither Earned (the brand paid for it) nor Paid (the brand has surrendered the ability to craft the message to the extent they would via advertisements). It is also not Owned (the brand did not produce it). It is instead Sponsored.

Podcasts are a very common environment for sponsored media. There, the podcast host serves a similar function to an influencer (from the brand's point of view). Audio channels of influence are a natural fit for this kind of promotion as hosts can easily slip sponsored messages into their talk track, much like radio DJs have for years. It's easy to see other audio services or platforms such as Alexa Skills or Clubhouse providing forms of sponsored media in the near future.

The interesting generational shift has been away from paid media in favor of sponsored media. Although millennial and Gen Z consumers detest the overt commercialness of advertisements, they openly embrace most forms of sponsored media. For example, despite being intuitively and obviously aware that influencers are pushing commercial messages, a 2020 study from Kantar found that 44 percent of Gen Z women have bought a product because it was promoted by an influencer. This generation, which personifies anti-advertising sentiment, has embraced the idea that influencers exercise a level of shrewdness when it comes to choosing which brands they'll agree to promote. This makes these messages more trustworthy than advertisements, which anyone can pay to place. There are plenty of examples where influencers have broken their audience's trust and therefore lost hordes of followers. This ability to opt out of the marketing messages by simplifying unfollowing is a hallmark of the marketing that younger consumers embrace today.

I sometimes ask marketers, "If consumers were allowed to opt out of your marketing efforts, how many of them would you still reach?" If the answer scares you, it's probably time to reconsider your marketing plan before the #unsubscribe generation simply forgets about you.

Influencers and podcasters are not the only ones offering sponsored media to marketers. Media outlets have been experimenting for years now with similar offerings where internal creative groups at publishers help brands produce content that will appeal to their readers. Native advertising specifically jumped out to a hot start several years ago but ran headlong into Google. Unfortunately, as with paywalls, Google purposefully held this kind of content back by refusing to index it in search results. In fact, several media outlets in the United Kingdom were punished by Google for not willingly identifying and excluding native advertisements on their site from their Google search results. Thankfully, in this case Google issued a widespread change in 2019 by allowing media outlets to index their sponsored content with a new tag that simply identifies it as such. The content will now have a lesser but still relevant impact on search engine rankings, and the pages themselves have been indexed and findable in Google ever since.

Other forms of sponsored media have existed for decades, including advertorials in print magazines, product placements in Hollywood, and paid integrations in broadcast media. However, as media outlets have struggled in recent years, the frequency of these deals has risen. In fact, most large PR firms today tell their clients that truly earned opportunities are all but gone for branded product mentions on broadcast television. They instead push clients directly to paid integrations where the product is mentioned or showcased on-air in exchange for a sponsorship fee. At Lippe Taylor, we still earn a huge amount of editorial broadcast coverage, but there's no doubt it's gotten much harder with the rise of sponsored media.

Although sponsored media has made it more difficult to garner editorial coverage, it is a meaningful and valuable advancement in mass media offerings. Brands that are concerned with the declining impact of their advertising efforts should be repurposing dollars from those budgets into more sponsored content and paid integrations, as well as sponsored collaborations with influencers and creative departments at media outlets. We'll dig into this more when we talk about collaborating as a strategy in Chapter 6.

TAKING ON THE 4PS...THE MOST FAMOUS TROPE IN MARKETING

Many years ago at W2O Group, I introduced a concept called the 4As to describe how marketers could influence consumer behavior online (Awareness, Assessment, Action, Ambassador). Almost immediately, I was encouraged to position the 4As as "The New 4Ps." Doing so would lend credibility and intrigue, I was told. As the 4As took hold and new people joined the company, it became clear how easy it was to come up with four words that began with a common letter and were applicable to marketing. Soon enough, there were competing internal factions arguing whether the 4Ls, the 4Cs, or the 4Es would be better. Today, quickly scrolling through any marketing trade is likely to return myriad articles purporting to alter or improve on Jerome McCarthy's classic 4P framework (Product, Place, Promotion, Price).

The truth is, McCarthy's 1960s treatise on marketing for managers has stood the test of time. Even with all the dramatic disruption and evolution of society and marketing today, the 4Ps are still remarkably effective at describing the marketing mix. However, the role of marketing inside of companies has in fact changed dramatically. Speaking to trade magazine *The Drum* in 2021, Mastercard CMO Raja Rajamannar explained, "Marketing is becoming highly fragmented. Look at the classical definition of marketing from Philip Kotler about the 4Ps of marketing (product, price, place, promotion). Today, marketing doesn't handle product in most of the companies. Marketing doesn't handle any pricing and at most of the companies, marketing doesn't handle place which is logistics in most cases. They are barely hanging on to promotions, at best." (Note: Philip Kotler popularized the 4P concept that McCarthy coined.)[26]

This book is written for today's marketers as they struggle to rethink their plans for tomorrow. Therefore, it will NOT purport to alter the 4P framework. Rather, the primary focus falls within McCarthy's third P, Promotions, which has become somewhat inexplicably intertwined with advertising as if one and the same. This focus on promotions is because, if marketers intend to retain their grasp on at least some element of the 4Ps, they are running out of time to evolve their approaches.

Promotion, as outlined in McCarthy's original book, is described by the acronym AIDA (which he relates to the famous opera of the same name for easy recall). AIDA stands for the four objectives of Promotion, which are:

1. Gain **A**ttention
2. Hold **I**nterest
3. Arouse **D**esire
4. Obtain **A**ction

In McCarthy's telling, Promotion has its roots in early merchants and shopkeepers who would stand outside their stalls and shout to gain attention, hold interest, arouse desire, and obtain action. As the world grew and it became less realistic for shopkeepers to yell at every person they wanted to reach, mass media became their vehicle, and McCarthy acknowledges advertising as one way of reaching people.

---

26   Kenneth Hein, "3 Actionable Insights with…Mastercard's Raja Rajamannar," *The Drum*, February 10, 2021, https://www.thedrum.com/ news/2021/02/10/3-actionable-insights-with-mastercards-raja-rajamannar.

The analogy of a shopkeeper yelling at people in a town square could not be more apt. Despite all of Big Advertising's protestations about making ads that people *want* to see, the truth is, there's nothing the shopkeeper can yell that isn't initially irritating. People don't want to be yelled at, and they don't want to be interrupted by advertising.

SOCIAL MEDIA DROVE A NEW KIND OF INTEGRATED MARKETING

In early 2008, I was the Managing Director of Interactive Media at an independent PR firm called CarryOn Communications. At that time, I was considered one of the country's foremost leaders in social media marketing, largely because very few people had committed themselves to it as a career choice (commitment is a concept we'll return to in Chapter 5 when we discuss the dilemmas facing brand marketers). Therefore, I boarded a plane from sunny Los Angeles and touched down in the bitter cold of Golden, Colorado, to join an integrated agency team (IAT) meeting for our client, Coors Light. Andy England was the Chief Marketing Officer at Coors Light, and he was a luminary in integrated marketing approaches. This meeting had been scheduled as an in-person meeting of the IAT, consisting of my agency (public relations) along with DraftFCB (advertising), Avenue A / Razorfish (digital marketing), and the Integer Group (promotions).

Andy kicked off the two-day summit by getting right down to it. "We're here because we expect a 360 degree campaign this year. That means every agency partner is expected to behave like they're part of the brand team." Andy went on to explain the objectives for the year with an emphasis on launching the brand's new packaging, which included an innovative new design that turned blue to signal when the beer was cold enough to drink.

The part that still stands out in my mind today, however, is what he did next.

"You all have your budgets for the year," he said. "None of you are getting any more. So I want you to work together knowing that all of your success depends on us meeting the objectives I've just laid out." In other words, if you have ideas that encroach on another agency's territory, that's fine. But you won't get any extra budget for it. And if you want this year to be seen as a success, you will work toward collective metrics instead of working in your own siloes.

The result was remarkable. To this day, it still stands out as the best interagency collaboration I've ever experienced. My agency was quickly identified as the "lead" agency for social media, largely because I was the only person in the group who had committed myself to social media entirely. It was also a time when most agencies dismissed social media as a novelty rather than a marketing pillar to fight over. That didn't mean other agencies checked out, though. Razorfish developed a fantastic app that used a Facebook Maps feature to help friends meet at local bars. The Integer Group leveraged Facebook Events, and DraftFCB mocked a series of engaging posts for MySpace. Of all the agencies, it was clear the advertising agency (DraftFCB) was grappling the most with treating everyone's ideas as equal.

Nevertheless, we developed several campaign ideas in total collaboration, one of which, named Cold Front, was a social media-led campaign (meaning there would be no major advertising support). The campaign included faking an avalanche in the Rocky Mountains that somehow turned into a glacial iceberg and floated along rivers all the way to Manhattan. In fact, we actually built a fake glacier that appeared on the nightly news floating in the East River. Social media promoted the supposed path of the iceberg as it floated to New York. We even convinced the media buying team to repurpose paid media dollars to support the campaign with mock weather reports on Weather.com and other sites.

Source: Ross Schneiderma, "A Coors Sponsored Cold Front" *The New York Times*, April 27. 2009.

The level of interagency collaboration was so rare that when we pitched *The New York Times* on the campaign, the article spent more time remarking on the collaboration between agencies than the campaign itself. Somewhat comically, the creative director from our advertising partner was quoted in the article as saying, "This new world we live in, it's something we're learning to live with."[27]

Meanwhile, the integrated effort delivered the most successful new packaging launch in Coors Light history. Sales velocity and

27   Stuart Elliott, "Coors Light Uses Cold to Turn up Heat on Rivals," *The New York Times*, April 27, 2009, https://www.nytimes.com/2009/04/27/business/media/27adnewsletter1.html.

distribution both increased more than 3 percent, and we gained five points against Bud Light in market share. We also attracted over a million new fans without spending a dollar on Facebook ads (those were the days). After the campaign wrapped, one of the senior leaders from DraftFCB called to recruit me. "Why would people want advertising in their social media?" I asked.

Despite this being a tremendous collaboration among the agencies, DraftFCB had struggled the most with this new way of working—a struggle that was best summarized when their creative director told *The New York Times* they were "learning to live with it." Despite the campaign being developed by a fully integrated agency team, the most noteworthy contribution for the advertising agency was to bring forth a long list of **concepts** that would make for good advertisements. Meanwhile, the differentiating **ideas** came from my agency (we delivered the Cold Front concept) and Razorfish (their execution of Code Blue turned a TV concept into an idea people would engage with online). More on this distinction between advertising concepts and marketing ideas later, but this description of the dynamics between agencies is so common that it's practically de facto across the industry. However, because few clients enforce truly equal status among the agencies, the differentiating ideas often get vetoed or mutilated by advertising agencies when given the chance.

Almost twelve years after that experience, Marcelo Pascoa, now Vice-President for Marketing at Coors, was quoted in another article in *The New York Times*. This one was headlined "Pandemic Brings Change to 'Bloated' Ad Industry,"[28] and Marcelo aired his grievances at the advertising industry: "This is an industry that

---

28 "'A Big Correction': Pandemic Brings Change to 'Bloated' Ad Industry," *The New York Times*, last modified June 28, 2020, https://www.nytimes.com/2020/07/28/business/media/coronavirus-pandemic-advertising-industry.html.

is constantly talking about wanting to transform itself, but that is also constantly sticking to very traditional approaches," he said. With twelve years to prepare, it's safe to say we've seen the extent of transformation that Big Advertising is willing to embrace.

THE DANGEROUS ALLURE OF ITERATING AN OLD MODEL

What could Bloomberg have done differently with half a billion dollars? Much more. (Please pardon the cliffhanger; more on this in Chapter 6.) However, once he had committed to an advertising-led approach, many subsequent choices were essentially preordained.

With an advertising-led approach, the opportunity to repurpose creative assets from TV commercials is impossibly seductive. You've spent so much time strategizing and so much money producing the commercial that it seems natural that other marketing assets should simply be repurposed from there. Not surprisingly, this idea has its roots in the same halls where "advertising isn't dying; only the channels are changing" can be heard. For Big Advertising, this worldview means continuing business as usual with a few tweaks for modern consumers. Research is conducted in largely the same, artificial ways. A preciously guarded creative process delivers a *Big Idea*, and the media plan is based on where you can force the most people to view your ad. The planning overwhelmingly occurs in Madison Avenue-style conference rooms among people who have no idea how different they are from the people they're trying to influence across America. (More on what audiences want in Chapter 4.)

But what's the inevitable result of recycling a TV commercial into a pre-roll ad for YouTube? An irritated viewer's rising anxiety levels as they wait to mash the Skip button. Why? Because the kind of video that works on YouTube is very different from the videos that are most likely to be produced by established ad agency people and processes.

More importantly, because the advertising process assumes the ability to force people to watch your video, the entire way of thinking about the content is skewed against the viewer. Thirty- and sixty-second commercials are scripted under the presumption that people will be at attention for a full thirty or sixty seconds. The unfortunate truth is that for years now, people have tuned out when ads came on, but today's time-strapped and impatient audiences go a step further—angrily tapping the Skip button the moment it's available to them.

Advertisers who were shaped by the norms of the 1990s, 2000s, and 2010s were spoiled by the ability to force people to watch their ads. It was totally acceptable, even preferable, to make the ad overwhelmingly self-serving.

Consumers had little choice in the matter: if they wanted to read a magazine or watch something on TV, they were going to be subjected to the ad. This decades-long state of affairs raises a larger point.

The people and processes that evolved to create advertising do not produce the kind of marketing programs that offer good experiences for modern audiences; they produce the kind of marketing programs that are effective at selling products, but only *if* the consumer can be forced to view them. However, as consumers have increasingly avoided, blocked, and eliminated ads, the industry that creates them has remained largely unchanged. This is the danger of iterating an old model. New advertising agencies are started every year. But the lion's share of the advertising industry is still dominated by a small number of holding companies that prescribe processes defined by their success in the past. Even the hundreds of advertising startups that have spun off from the holding companies tend to follow eerily similar processes, all while proclaiming their uniqueness.

Since the 1950s, when psychologists feared the power of subliminal messages in advertising, the public's relationship to media and advertisement has shifted dramatically. Cannes awards aside, Big Advertising can no longer get away with deceiving anyone of its own greatness. Brand marketers don't get promoted by receiving Cannes Lions; they get promoted by building brands. And the fact is, people are so fed up with advertising that they are paying money to avoid it. In other words, consumers have taken matters into their own hands and are simply opting out of their relationship with Big Advertising.

CHAPTER 3

HOW MEDIA COMPANIES ARE REINVENTING THEMSELVES

When people think about the disruption of media, they usually conjure up images of declining newspaper circulations, empty evening news desks, and shuttered magazines. In reality, even the shiny and cool digital-native media outlets have proven unable to build a sustainable business while Google and Facebook gobble up all the ad revenue.

Mashable, Buzzfeed, Vice, and other digital-native publishers—the supposed darlings of the millennial generation—faced layoffs and worse as their VC-fueled horizons came due. In 2017, Mashable sold to Ziff Davis for a fraction of its former valuation;[29] Buzzfeed laid off more than 40 of its 250 journalists at BuzzFeed News in 2019;[30] that same year, Vice Media announced 10 per-

---

29 Elahe Izadi, "With Cuts at Vice, Quartz and BuzzFeed, Even Media's Savviest Digital Players Are Hurting," *The Washington Post*, May 19, 2020, https://www.washingtonpost.com/lifestyle/media/with-cuts-at-vice-quartz-buzzfeed-even-medias-savviest-digital-players-are-hurting/2020/05/19/f15d3dde-96e9-11ea-91d7-cf4423d47683_story.html.

30 Jaclyn Peiser, "BuzzFeed's First Round of Layoffs Puts an End to Its National News Desk," *The New York Times*, January 25, 2019, https://www.nytimes.com/2019/01/25/business/media/buzzfeed-layoffs.html.

cent of its workforce would be laid off after the company lost $50 million, and in 2020, it laid off another 150 employees.[31] These companies were heralded as the future of publishing but fell victim to the same trends as their predecessors.

The correlated desperation for advertising revenue produces a familiar experience for readers. Consider, for instance, a relatable example. Let's say you want quick help finding recipes to fit a certain theme—Spanish tapas. There, at the top of your Google search results is a tantalizingly perfect Top Tapas Recipes list. It seems to be calling your name. So you click on it and start reading.

However, rather than quickly finding top tapas recipes, you are instead subjected to endless jibber jabber about how important tapas recipes are, why the author decided to write this Top Tapas Recipes list, how the best Top Tapas Recipes list is the key to a romantic evening, and all sorts of other nonsense. You know why that's there? Because that keyword stuffing was necessary to get this particular Top Tapas Recipes list placed at the top of your Google search results.

Okay, so you've finally made it past the gibberish, and you're ready for some tapas inspo—bring on the top tapas recipes. But what do you see instead? Now it's a Gallery or a Slideshow instead of an actual list. Instead of being free to quickly scan and see which of the recipes might appeal to you, the site plunges you into a tedious march of clicking and page loading to see the headline for each recipe (viewing the full recipe requires you to click and load again). In between every second or third recipe, you're interrupted by advertisements for cookware, and to add insult

---

31   Todd Spangler, "Vice Media to Axe 10 Percent of Staff, Laying Off about 250 Employees amid Revenue Slowdown," *Variety*, February 1, 2019, https://variety.com/2019/digital/news/vice-media-layoffs-250-employees-1203125890/.

to injury, you're made to wait extra long while the slides with the advertisements load due to all the privacy-trodding cookies that are loading in the background.

Why does this happen? It happens because both you and Google expected your list of tapas recipes to be free, and according to marketing consultants Solve Media, the likelihood of you clicking on a banner ad (which generates much higher revenues for the publisher than simple impressions) is lower than the likelihood you will summit Mount Everest. Therefore, the publisher that wrote your list of tapas recipes is trying to wring every possible cost-per-impression out of loading and reloading the banner ads from your one website visit.

Before the collapse of the media industry, leading news and media outlets had editors whose entire jobs centered on optimizing the layout of their content. Maureen Lippe, who held editorial leadership roles at publications such as *Vogue* and *Harper's Bazaar*, describes the height of this attention to detail by saying, "In those days, we knew the exact positioning, color, and font choice could be the difference between people engaging versus glossing over. We were paid to engage them. In fact, we got reader scores for our pages, and we agonized over those details."

Just like Bezos at Amazon, they were agonizing over how to make the experience totally *frictionless* for readers. However, one of the unfortunate results of the media business model collapsing was the ensuing desperation to display as many ads as possible. Thus, rather than presenting the top tapas recipes in a straightforward manner, they force readers to reload the banner ads again and again. They know it's a terrible experience, but advertisers are willing to pay for it, never mind that by the time you've found an interesting recipe, you're probably too tired to get the pots and pans out of the cupboard.

This kind of underhanded behavior, undertaken at the expense of the reader, would never happen in a world where media outlets prioritized their own audiences (readers or viewers) over their advertisers. Thankfully, however, that shift in priority is already underway. This is good news for consumers, as a 2018 report from the American Press Institute explained, "Reorienting to focus on subscription revenues requires...focus on the needs of readers instead of advertisers."

Although much has been made of *The New York Times*'s subscription revenue overshadowing its advertiser revenue, the chaos of 2020 accelerated this trend among their peers across the media landscape. In fact, a senior executive at Condé Nast recently told me that in 2020, more than 60 percent of the company's revenue came from consumers rather than advertisers.

FIGHTING BACK AGAINST THE DUOPOLY

In a private showdown that was later widely publicized, Rupert Murdoch, the infamous media magnate and owner of News Corp, took Mark Zuckerberg to task for Facebook's role in destroying journalism. Murdoch, who years previously had tried to surreptitiously tank Facebook by deploying black hat legal teams to propagate false stories of sexual predation on the platform, may not be the mission-driven savior we typically imagine.[32] But he did have a point. In the years to follow that 2016 sit-down between billionaires, Facebook has started making concessions to publishers. However, they have been too few and far between, with regulators and disgruntled journalists finally labeling the social media site as public enemy number one.

This trend has continued and gained its first serious threat to Facebook in 2020 when Apple judged that discontent among consumers about Facebook, coupled with the role it played in destroying journalism, was enough justification for a corporate declaration of war. In an unprecedented move, Apple announced it would prompt iPhone users to decide whether they want to opt in or out of Facebook's advertising crawlers.

In his speech announcing the update, Apple CEO Tim Cook accused Facebook of asking "'how much can we get away with?' when they need to be asking 'what are the consequences?'" and further explained his company's decision to hand consumers the option of opting out of Facebook's advertising trackers by saying, "In a moment of rampant disinformation and conspiracy theories juiced by algorithms, we can no longer turn a blind eye to a theory of technology that says all engagement is good engagement, the

---

32   Nicholas Thompson and Fred Vogelstein, "Inside the Two Years That Shook Facebook—and the World," *Wired*, February 12, 2018, https://www.wired.com/story/inside-facebook-mark-zuckerberg-2-years-of-hell/.

longer the better, and all with the goal of collecting as much data as possible."

It's an important move. When asked whether they would choose to opt out of advertisers tracking their online behaviors, more than 80 percent of respondents in the *Friction Fatigue Report* said yes. To believe Apple's move was motivated by purely missionary purposes would be naive. Their mercenary instincts were at least equal parts responsible for the move, with Apple tiring of Facebook playing competitor. In fact, it also underscores a broader discontent among innovators and technologists toward companies that rely on advertising, rather than product innovation, for their income. This sentiment is particularly apparent in the historically product- and engineer-led Silicon Valley where the outsized influence of Big Advertising has enabled startups with unremarkable ideas or capabilities to raise millions of dollars in capital on the promise that they could target people with ads like Facebook and Google do.

Apple co-founder Steve Wozniak expressed this feeling at the Festival of Marketing in 2016. "Google primarily makes money off advertising, while Apple makes [it from] good products—there's a big difference," Wozniak said.[33] He went on to say that the best marketing is "understanding what people want in products and being honest when talking about how much it is truly worth to them."

It is ironic, therefore, that Google preceded Apple's big move with a move of its own. By announcing in 2020 that the Google Chrome browser would no longer support third-party cookies,

---

33   Thomas Hobbs, "The Best Brands Are 'Built on Product Not Advertising,' Says Apple Co-founder Steve Wozniak," MarketingWeek, October 6, 2016, https://www.marketingweek.com/the-best-brands-are-built-on-product-not-advertising-says-apple-co-founder-steve-wozniak/.

Google was taking a shot at Facebook's pixel tracking. Taken together with Apple's announcement, these are two serious blows to the influence of Big Advertising over tech. However, they may be coming too late. A wave of new regulations and legislation are being debated around the world, any of which will rock the online advertising world with Facebook and Google being the biggest losers.

As governments take steps to limit how these companies monetize media content and personal data, they will be severely limited in their ability to target ads. This will destroy the basis for huge swaths of the online advertising industry. And if governments make good on current legislation that would require Google and Facebook to compensate publishers for content displayed on their networks, the cash infusion will undoubtedly lead to even stronger resistance among those audience-focused media outlets to bend to advertisers.

It's easy to see Apple's move and the wave of government action as the vanguard in the fight against the duopoly. But it was the media who exercised their power of the pen to create the conditions for action. Although News Corp is adamant it only deployed its executives and its lawyers in the fight against Facebook—publicly swearing that its journalists have remained impartial—the news media has played a major role in swinging public perception against Facebook and even Google. Calls to pay publishers when content is shared or viewed through their platforms have intensified in recent years with the two-pronged attack of the Cambridge Analytica scandal and the explosion of fake news being used to demonstrate why Google and Facebook must be held accountable. It's a stark reminder of why you should never lose sight of who's holding the pen that crafts the narrative.

With these new changes to privacy laws and protocols, performance marketing will take a dramatic hit, and media outlets will be even further incentivized to cater to their audiences over advertisers. After all, the audiences were always a media company's most valuable asset. Whether they were selling goods and services directly to those consumers, or merchandising them to advertisers, the audience is a media company's lifeblood. Speaking on this topic in early 2021, Sebastian "Seb" Tomich told me, "For us, it comes down to mutual audience obsession. As media outlets, we have to be obsessed with our audience so that they will also be obsessed with us." Seb should know; as the Global Head of Advertising for *The New York Times*, he has played a key role in developing the company's strategy.

Facebook and Google have largely avoided regulation and legislation by claiming they are an impartial third party. They do not "obsess" over the audiences' interests—they merely provide a forum where those audiences can do as they please. However, this claim is under fire from multiple perspectives now with public interest groups calling on the platforms to monitor hate speech and governments calling on them to respect users' privacy and share their profits with content producers. As these changes take hold, they will undermine the duopoly's business model. Once again, media outlets will have the upper hand in understanding their audiences. And once again, those audiences will become extremely valuable assets.

It's an exciting moment where innovation by media outlets could set them apart from their competition. Let's now unpack how media outlets are adjusting, beginning with how they are resetting internal objectives.

PIVOTING TO AUDIENCE REVENUE

In October 2019, Condé Nast CEO Robert Lynch having only taken the role in April, announced his plan to pivot the company's strategy away from advertising revenue in favor of audience revenue. By June 2020, due to the pandemic's acceleration of existing trends, the company's advertising revenues had dropped 45 percent year over year. By late 2020, across all brands and imprints, from the likes of *Architectural Digest* and *Vogue* to *GQ, Vanity Fair,* and *Wired,* the company boasted more than 70 million print readers, nearly 400 million digital readers, and upward of 450 million on social platforms. And by the close of 2020, those audiences made up 65 percent of revenue for Condé Nast. On a base of $1.2 billion in revenue, that was a significant shift from the year prior.

Although it may be difficult to parse how much of this shift was pandemic-led and how much was driven by the new strategy, Lynch's articulation of refocusing on audience revenue has become the defining theme of the media industry. When Reuters ran a survey of media companies in thirty-two countries, asking which revenue stream would be most important going forward, half answered "reader revenue," followed by 35 percent for "reader and advertising revenue" and only 15 percent for "advertising revenue."[34] Responses to the same survey in 2021 shifted even more to reader revenue.

But this latest swing wasn't the first time Condé Nast had thought about deriving more income from its audiences.

In 2011, they were the first major publisher to offer subscriptions on the iPad, for *The New Yorker,* part of a larger trend that led

---

34 Nic Newman, "Journalism, Media, and Technology Trends and Predictions 2020," Reuters Institute, January 9, 2020, https://reutersinstitute.politics.ox.ac.uk/journalism-media-and-technology-trends-and-predictions-2020.

them to join five publishers in offering content for Android on Samsung's Galaxy Tab. Digital subscriptions were offered as add-ons or bundles with print subscriptions. The challenge at that time was consumers' continued reluctance to pay for content. However, through extensive testing and the proverbial learning through failure, Condé Nast and other publishers have designed a more nuanced approach to designing paywalls. Thankfully, the retraining offered by Spotify and Netflix has influenced consumers' broader willingness to pay for content.

As a result, there are several approaches being embraced by publishers as they pivot to subscription revenue. Which direction they choose depends on the goals of the publisher, from revenue targets to the quality of the experience they'd like to offer audiences. Consider a 2 × 2 landscape where breadth of content is the y-axis with quantity of free content on the x-axis. The all-or-nothing approach taken by outlets such as The Athletic or *The Economist* offers low breadth, low quantity of free articles. The metered offering—high breadth of content with low number of free articles—is used by Medium.com, *The Boston Globe*, and *The Washington Post*. Low breadth but high quantity of free content is gated content, with ESPN or YouTube Premium as basic examples. Finally, there's the no-paywall approach that BuzzFeed, Vox, Politico, and *The Guardian* have implemented, relying on advertising, sponsored content, and donations. You can probably imagine numerous versions and variations to this rather simplified two-dimensional model.

THE PAY WALL DESIGN SPACE

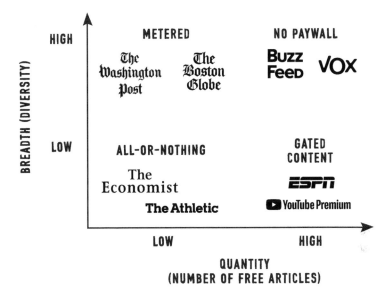

NOTES. MEDIA COMPANIES, SUCH AS THE NYT, THAT HAVE A POROUS PAYWALL DO NOT ENTIRELY FALL INTO ONE OF THESE 2X2 BUCKETS. THE NYT PAYWALL OFFERING (AS OF 2019) IS HIGH BREATH AND MEDIUM QUANTITY IN TERMS OF THESE TWO PARAMETERS

Source: Sinan Aral and Paramveer S. Dhillon, "Digital Paywall Design: Implications for Content Demand and Subscriptions," *Management Science*.

Regardless of the specific paywall strategy, it's important to note across the industry it's working. And it's reorienting the definition of who the customer is for media outlets. *The New York Times*, Gannett, and News Corp each reported growth in the number of subscriptions in early 2020. In fact, *The New York Times* reported a record-breaking uptick (more than 39 percent growth compared to Q1 of 2019) of 587,000 net new digital subscriptions. Gannett saw a 29 percent growth in subscriptions compared to last year to about 863,000 digital subscriptions. News Corp's Dow Jones properties saw a 20 percent growth in digital-only subscribers to over 2.5 million, which amounted to a 15 percent growth in digital-only subscribers alone at *The Wall Street Journal*. The *Financial Times* broke through its one million subscriber target, while *The Guardian* returned to profit in 2019—its first in nearly two decades—thanks to one million reader contributions spanning three years.

In 2000, reader subscriptions accounted for 26 percent of *The New York Times*'s revenue. Today, it's 70 percent. "We're a reader-supported institution, driven by people like you, who believe in truth and independence, rigor and fact," wrote Jodi Kantor, one of the reporters who broke the culture-changing Epstein story.[35]

Reader subscriptions can provide a steady base of revenue in volatile advertising climates. Jon Slade, Chief Commercial Officer at the *Financial Times*, said in a Reuters report, "Growth engines, reader revenue specifically, has very positive prospects; advertising revenue remains a major concern."[36]

The media outlets' position on reader revenue and advertising revenue matters a great deal. We're moving from a world that for many years has defined the customer as advertisers to now defining it as audiences, which means that we're going to get a very different type of experience from media outlets.

PUBLISHER CREATIVE STUDIOS

Even while audience revenues are getting a nice shot in the arm, publishers aren't completely giving up on advertising revenue. They just don't want the advertising to turn off their audiences.

---

35   David Leonhardt, "Thank You, Readers," *The New York Times*, November 23, 2017, https://www. nytimes.com/2017/11/23/opinion/thanksgiving-note-new-york-times.html.

36   Newman, "Journalism, Media, and Technology Trends and Predictions 2020."

To that end, the future lies in the growth of publisher creative departments, and some media outlets are already building these in-house creative teams. These creative departments are often staffed with a mix of people from editorial, production, and agency backgrounds, and their pitch is that a media outlet's internal creative studio is better at engaging that outlet's audience than any agency or in-house creative could ever be. Although this trend has its appeal, most brands will no doubt still need an agency of some kind, working with the publisher's creative teams, to balance the brand's objectives with the publisher's and to ensure some level of consistency across publishers. Even so, advertising agencies are ill-equipped to be these partners. This is best illustrated by a widely circulated example of a client-agency agreement between DDB (a top-ten ad agency worldwide) and its client, Avis Car Rental:

AVIS RENT A CAR ADVERTISING PHILOSOPHY

1. AVIS WILL NEVER KNOW AS MUCH ABOUT ADVERTISING AS DDB, AND DDB WILL NEVER KNOW AS MUCH ABOUT THE RENT A CAR BUSINESS AS AVIS.

2. THE PURPOSE OF THE ADVERTISING IS TO PERSUADE THE FREQUENT BUSINESS RENTER (WHETHER ON A BUSINESS TRIP, A VACATION TRIP OR RENTING AN EXTRA CAR AT HOME) TO TRY AVIS.

3. A SERIOUS ATTEMPT WILL BE MADE TO CREATE ADVERTISING WITH FIVE TIMES THE EFFECTIVENESS (SEE #2 ABOVE) OF THE COMPETITION'S ADVERTISING.

4. TO THIS END, AVIS WILL APPROVE OR DISAPPROVE, NOT TRY TO IMPROVE, ADS WHICH ARE SUBMITTED. ANY CHANGES SUGGESTED BY AVIS MUST BE GROUNDED ON A MATERIAL OPERATING DEFECT (A WRONG UNIFORM FOR EXAMPLE).

5. TO THIS END, DDB WILL ONLY SUBMIT FOR APPROVAL THOSE ADS WHICH THEY, AS AN AGENCY, RECOMMEND. THEY WILL NOT "SEE WHAT AVIS THINKS OF THAT ONE."

6. MEDIA SELECTION SHOULD BE THE PRIMARY RESPONSIBILITY OF DDB. HOWEVER, DDB IS EXPECTED TO TAKE THE INITIATIVE TO GET GUIDANCE FROM AVIS IN WEIGHTING OF MARKETS OR SPECIAL SITUATIONS, PARTICULARLY IN THOSE AREAS WHERE COLD NUMBERS DO NOT INDICATE THE REAL PICTURE. MEDIA JUDGMENTS ARE OPEN TO DISCUSSION. THE CONVICTION SHOULD PREVAIL.

COMPROMISES SHOULD BE AVOIDED.

Source: Jim Thornton and Troy Warfield, "Avis Budget resurrects DDB's 'six point contract,'" *Campaign*, June 25, 2014.

This agreement was written in the 1960s, so it's easy to dismiss the agency's hubris as a relic of a bygone era...except that it was resurrected during agency negotiations and reaffirmed in 2014! Very little has changed for Big Advertising even while the surrounding world has moved on. These agencies often still view compromise with their clients as creative failure and believe they hold a monopoly on the business of persuasion. Meanwhile, the world around them has moved on. Reinvented media outlets have finally divorced themselves from the lumbering albatross of Big Advertising and are now looking for a new kind of partner. These partners will not presume to know everything about how to reach the publisher's audience. In fact, the best creative thinkers for these new kinds of programs will not think like advertising creatives at all. They will instead think of ideas that are worth reading about because the media outlet won't allow marketers to interrupt their audiences like they used to.

Ultimately, this will lead to a better marketing experience for consumers, but there's no doubt it will also lead to less marketing overall. In 2020, Forrester estimated the advertising industry would lose 52,000 jobs due to the pandemic but that only half would return.

Publishers are betting their internal creative teams can do a better job of engaging their audiences than ad agencies can. And they're okay with losing business from brand marketers who don't want to play by their rules. To illustrate the point, Meredith Kopit Levien, Chief Executive of *The New York Times*, said, "We will have a larger concentration of advertisers in smaller numbers of categories." In other words, less space dedicated to advertising by fewer advertisers.

In place of advertising, sponsored media—born of collaboration between the brand and the publisher's creative team—will blossom. An example of this was Shell Corporation's "Future of Energy" project, which led to one million viewers in New York and Houston (38 percent above their benchmark mobile engagement) and more than 12,000 augmented reality interactions with magic windows detailing Shell's path to net-zero emissions by 2070. This collaboration was produced by *The New York Times*'s T Brand Studio, which has produced sponsored media with HP, Facebook Watch, Burberry, Cartier, Dropbox, Dove, and many others.

The key for T Brand Studio is that much of what this group does would historically have been done by an ad agency. Now *The New York Times* is doing it themselves because *The New York Times* is better at producing content that their audience is actually interested in. Their position is, if you want to reach our readers, you'll trust us on how to best do that. This pitch will increasingly take root with brand marketers, and agencies that want to succeed will operate in collaboration mode instead of demanding authoritarian control over the content that gets produced. It is undoubtedly too much to expect Big Advertising to come further in the space of a few years than it was able in the decades between DDB's initial contract with Avis and 2014.

WHY IT MATTERS FOR MARKETERS

First and foremost, it's important to be aware that media outlets are in the midst of redefining their customer as the audience instead of...well...you, the marketer. Second, it's important to realize they are flipping their business model in many ways. Historically, media outlets would *create* editorial content and *sell space* for advertising. They rarely sold the editorial and rarely created the advertising.

Today, that's all changing. Media outlets are offering to create branded content (advertising) and integrate you into their editorial (for a fee). Although this offers interesting new opportunities, the challenge for marketers is twofold.

1. ATOMIZATION

Most marketers work with an agency to make a relatively small number of ads and then pay dozens of media outlets to place them. Those outlets are now limiting their ad space and proposing to make the ads for you, instead of your agency. On the surface, it's a logical proposition: the media company knows their audience best and is an expert at producing content that resonates with them (although the journalists who create that relevance are not actually the same people making your branded content). However, most marketers seek some level of consistency in their messaging and content. How will that be achieved when different media outlets are all producing content according to their own standards for their own audiences?

And most marketers are accustomed to working with two advertising partners: one that makes the ads and one that places the ads. How will they handle a dozen different media outlets that all want direct access to the marketer? And can they afford to keep an agency in place while also paying creative and content teams at the media outlets to make their content?

2. AUTHENTICITY

Perhaps the most famous "A" word of the last decade, authenticity has been used to define the millennial generation in every conference room from New York to Mumbai. Achieving balance between being authentic to both the brand and the audience in an environment where every media outlet exerts much more control over the content being distributed among their network will be a challenge. Additionally, while there's no doubt the younger generations have accepted sponsored media as their preferred format for commercial messages, there's always the lurking risk that branded content or paid integrations will become too commercial and turn off the audience like advertising has.

Despite these challenges, it's important to acknowledge the new direction the industry is taking and to think about how it affects your promotional plans. Marketers should be making serious strides to diminish the role of traditional advertising in their marketing mix while pursuing sponsored media collaborations instead. This will require more time and effort than simply buying ads, but the result will be much greater engagement and relevance with consumers.

This shift may appear innovative or even revolutionary today, but in the very near future it will be the only path to success. This is because, across dozens of industries, consumers have grown fond of being the customer again. Everything from retail to insurance, healthcare to financial services, and music publishing to higher education bears the marks of "consumerization." That same trend is now coming for marketing. Consumers expect to dictate the terms of how they experience marketing. So the question becomes, what kind of marketing *do* they want?

CHAPTER 4

WHAT KIND OF MARKETING DO CONSUMERS WANT?

In Chapter 1, we discussed psychological reactance, which is the innate rejection of anyone or anything that attempts to limit our behavioral freedom—in other words, our natural inclination to reject anything that presumes to tell us what to do or think.

This concept describes much of the consumer backlash to old-school advertising, and the inverse describes much of how consumers want to experience marketing. That is, they want marketing on their own terms, not the advertiser's. This is reinforced by their affection for influencers—consumers control the experience because they can opt out anytime by simply unfollowing.

I spent the first six or seven years of my career as a social media consultant to top marketing leaders. In fact, my very first client was the CMO at Virgin Megastore, who was an innovator in embracing social media. During that time, I spoke regularly at conferences about the coming revolution of social media and how citizen journalism and peer-to-peer influence would upend the media and advertising industries.

Fast forward fifteen years, and I'm now the CEO of Lippe Taylor, one of the most iconic agencies in New York City. Along the way, at an agency called W2O Group, I was responsible for building what was at the time the largest social media analytics team in our industry with a hundred data scientists and analysts working for me. We worked with top marketers in companies ranging from Nike to Intel to P&G to Pfizer. Almost 100 percent of the data we analyzed came from consumer behavior in social media.

None of this career path I'm describing was by design. In fact, I stumbled into it because I was passionate about the opportunities social media posed for societal discourse, including marketing as well as politics, healthcare, education, and gaming, among other things.

One of my earliest qualifications as a social media marketing consultant was having been born at the right time. I was also among the oldest of the millennial generation—meaning I was ideally positioned to both participate in these social media trends from the beginning and also explain them to senior executives.

In 2018, as then-President of Lippe Taylor, I was leading a pitch to the Chief Customer Officer of Walmart's Jet.com. It was an intimidating prospect as someone who had made his career to that point on the backs of social media analytics and being a millennial whisperer. It was widely accepted that Walmart led the *Fortune* 500 in its prowess with analytics and Jet.com was renowned for having captured the hearts of millennials.

Our insights for this pitch largely pointed in the direction of fatigued consumers having a dissonant relationship with their favorite ecommerce sites. On the one hand, Amazon was a faceless and emotionless behemoth that served their needs. On the other hand, the retailers they were most passionate about were often niche and focused on offering a curated, personal experience.

I captured the room's attention by a similarly dissonant statement. "You want to reach millennial women living in big cities, and you think of them as social media mavens," I said matter-of-factly. "But the truth is, these women *under*-index in every category of social media engagement—posts, comments, shares, clicks—except for one: emojis. That means, with the exception of emojis, they are spending *less* time than the average American engaging in social media."

It was clear that I had their attention. Social media owed practically all of its societal prominence to millennial women. How was it that this cohort now engaged the least? The truth is, they were growing up and getting older. Many had married, had children, were caring for aging relatives, had taken roles in their communities, or become busier at work—often a combination of these. With compounding commitments, it made sense that they over-indexed in emojis—a fast, low-effort interaction—and that the only time they engaged more generally was very late at night.

"Now can you guess which emoji they use most?" No one in the room could. So I revealed the most-used emoji was the weary face 😩—an image that is defined as "a distraught-looking emoji with an open mouth and crescent-shaped eyes. Appears to have given up." Millennial women were overwhelmed. And they were 138 percent more likely to use the weary face emoji than the average American.

Adding to the drama, I then proceeded to reveal that their top keywords—those they used most often when posting on social media—were *time, people, family*, and *love*. The second, third, and fourth most common keywords seemed to align with the emojis rounding out their top-ten list: 🖤🤍😭🦋.

This drove home the dissonance in their online experience. Millennial women were using social media mostly to talk about their family and were acknowledging how overwhelmed they were. This was not the time for a big marketing program that required them to take action. Nor was it the time to interrupt them and make them watch an advertisement. Our recommendation was to make their lives easier—improved delivery options, curated offerings from friendly faces they could trust, and a streamlined list of brands and products to choose from (nobody has the time to cycle through a dozen listings for paper towels to figure out which assortment of rolls offers the best bang for the buck). In short, our goal was to make a connection by removing some of the friction from their lives. Thus, We Jet You was born.

In this case, data drove specific, actionable recommendations. At the close of the meeting, the CCO said, "You've got my attention. I've never seen anyone use data like this before." We learned almost immediately that we'd won the business. His first request as our new client was, "I'd like you to come down to Bentonville to teach us how to use data like you do."

I did go down to Bentonville, and we did do great work with Jet.com. However, that didn't stop them from plunging tens of millions of dollars into traditional advertising. Two years later, Walmart decided to shutter the company, internally pointing to myriad underlying issues that led to the retail app's failure. However, every conversation with senior executives in both the communications and marketing teams pointed to the advertising as having been particularly ineffective and wasteful.

Although this story highlights millennial women as consumers, the message applies universally: Friction-fatigued consumers want to experience marketing in a frictionless way. Now the test for brand marketers is to figure out how to bring clear variants of frictionless approaches into their marketing mix, whether Paid, Earned, Sponsored, or Owned. Because that's the kind of marketing consumers want.

There's no going back now. Tomorrow's consumer expects to experience marketing on her own terms. The rest of this chapter will explore the five expectations consumers have when it comes to experiencing marketing in the post-advertising era:

1. They expect to be heard.
2. They expect evidence for marketing claims.
3. They expect brands to be culturally relevant.
4. They expect to be engaged personally.
5. They expect brands to do more than selling products.

LISTENING TO THE VOICE OF THE CUSTOMER

In the late aughts, a wave of idea communities sprouted up in the *Fortune* 500 as a way of sourcing free ideas from consumers while also showing that the company cared what people thought. These idea communities are probably best exemplified by MyStarbucksIdea, which in its first five years in existence sourced over 150,000 ideas from consumers, roughly 300 of which were implemented by Starbucks. Everything from free Wi-Fi to the cult favorite PSL flavor (pumpkin spice latte), to the splash stick—that little green, plastic plunger to keep your Starbucks from spilling—were sourced from consumers submitting their ideas to Starbucks.

Although idea communities and open innovation challenges

(where companies invite the general public to help solve a problem) are well documented in several leading books, what's less well documented is the extraordinary value of passively listening to your consumers or other external audiences.

In 2012, my company relocated me from Austin to New York City. Although plenty of people can opine on the comparative charms of these two popular cities, the main reason I left the queso and sun-drenched capital of Texas for the concrete jungle was because I had taken on a multiyear, multimillion-dollar assignment to support Verizon CEO Lowell McAdam's executive mandate to understand the "voice of the customer" in their wireless division.

Voice-of-customer (VOC) initiatives had taken off in corporate America because people were expressing their opinions about products, brands, and companies in greater volume than ever before, and most of those opinions were visible online for anyone to see. Bezos himself was quoted as saying, "If you make customers unhappy in the physical world, they might each tell six friends. If you make customers unhappy on the internet, they can each tell 6,000." Companies had a choice to either listen to them (and improve) or ignore them and hope for the best.

Torod Neptune was the Head of Corporate Communications at Verizon when we kicked off this initiative. He explained to me, "We know a lot of people are unhappy when their calls drop, but there's nothing we can do to fix that problem right now, today. We're trying to listen for the signal in the noise of customer feedback where we can find opportunities to help make things better."

At Verizon, the CEO had made the VOC initiative one of his top-five priorities for the entire company. On the ground, this meant crunching more than one million social media posts every month from people who were complaining that their cell phone call had dropped. As Torod explained, we were looking for opportunities where Verizon could either help or learn something. Beyond social media, the program was designed to take every form of customer input—from handwritten feedback cards submitted at retail stores to transcriptions of customer service calls, merge it all together, and identify the issues that mattered to Verizon's customers. One of the most significant outcomes from this endeavor was the introduction of unlimited data plans. Without doubt, the largest volume of data came from social media posts mentioning Verizon.

Although most consumers don't realize the sheer magnitude of feedback many brands receive on social media, one thing is for certain—they expect brands to listen and respond to them. According to the *Friction Fatigue Report*, more than 75 percent of consumers who have posted about a brand online expect that brand to be listening to them. That number is even higher among frequent posters. "Listening to consumers" is also by far the number one response to the question "What would make you more likely to support a brand?" For context, nearly twice as many people picked listening over contributing to charitable causes.

Most people have heard of Kylie Jenner. Many have also heard of her company, Kylie Cosmetics, which sold a 51 percent stake to Coty, Inc. for $600 million after four years in business. What very few people know, however, is that Kylie Cosmetics' success was powered by a relatively small company called Seed Beauty, which takes cosmetic products from concept to consumer in less than two weeks. Laura Nelson is President at Seed Beauty. Speaking to Shopify in 2017, she explained the same phenomenon that Anne Talley was observing at Revlon but from the position of someone leading the revolution:

The democratization of beauty has been driven by two main factors, the first being social media. Information is being directly provided to the consumers so there's less filtering, less editing happening, and that really empowers the consumer to make really great purchasing decisions and get different perspectives directly from the brand. The second factor is ecommerce—consumers are able to buy those products online and brands are able to launch products when it works for them and their consumers. Traditionally, you had big retailers setting the pace.

The concepts for Seed Beauty are almost exclusively sourced by listening to consumers on social media. Therefore, when Kylie launches a new lip kit and it feels eerily on-trend, it's because it is. If something trended on social media last week, you can have it on your lips tomorrow.

This accelerated production and distribution timeline enabled Kylie Cosmetics to massively increase its share of wallet among Kylie fans who have become hooked on having the latest product. The key to its success was being of-the-moment in a way that no other brand could.

The problem for most established brands is that this kind of ongoing, always-on listening does not fit within typical planning cycles. Even for companies that have social listening programs in place, most of the decision makers wait until a monthly meeting where a PowerPoint deck reports top trending hashtags. By that time, Kylie Cosmetics has already turned around two new product SKUs and is preparing a third.

Although this example highlights the difference in agility between corporate behemoths and startups, it also points to the important difference between analyzing or researching your consumers and listening to them. Most good marketers appreciate the value of research. However, they also believe the research must be statistically significant, repeatable, and generalizable to a larger population. In other words, they STUDY their consumers. They research and analyze them in highly structured environments. Many of them believe they are listening to their customers by issuing surveys and performing focus groups, but these research environments all enable the marketer to set the frame for the conversation. You never hear what's really on the customer's mind outside the framework of your questionnaire.

When I talk with brands about listening, the analogy I draw is between visiting the gorilla exhibit in a zoo versus going on a jungle expedition with Jane Goodall. In one example, you're making a structured, time-bound trip with a specific purpose in mind—observing gorillas in the zoo. Everything about it is artificial. The gorilla's environment was constructed for your viewing, the timing of your visit is at your convenience, and you control the ability to initiate any stimulus in order to observe the gorilla's reaction. In the other example—trekking with gorillas in the wild—you are entering into the subject's world with no ability to control the parameters. Your only option is to listen, observe, and participate. In this context, you will learn how gorillas really behave, not just how they behave when you control all the parameters.

Trekking into the jungle with wild gorillas may be a hyperbolized analogy for listening to your customers, but it's an apt one. The brands that succeed with regular new product introductions, timely and relevant marketing campaigns, and a seemingly untouchable level of "brand love" all share one thing in common: they eschew annual market research reports in favor of truly listening to their customers on a regular, ongoing basis.

I've been making this argument for more than a decade now, and in most cases it has resonated. However, sometimes I run into objections, the most common of them being:

1. There are so many social media conversations that it's impossible to determine what really matters.
2. Even if we find gold while sifting through the river of social media, we're not operationally prepared to act on it quickly enough.
3. We understand our consumer well enough by now. We need to commit to the insights we have rather than changing the plan whenever something new comes up.
4. We need ideas that scale, and we can't commit major resources to something on the basis of a few social media posts.

Let me respond to all of these objections. AI and social media listening tools have enabled significant advances in finding the signal through the noise of social media, but none of the tools are enough. If you want to find gold in the river of social media, you need to commit to having a person whose job is listening to your consumer or stakeholders. Over time, this person will develop expertise and competency with their finger on the pulse of social media discourse, and they will then be prepared to use the tools effectively.

Once you've found gold, the unfortunate reality is that most big companies struggle with changing course or shifting resources quickly. This is why I always recommend keeping "dry powder" on hand so you can execute something outside the already approved plan. This dry powder can take the form of paid media budget reserved for opportunistic moments, agency or freelance resources who are already briefed on your brand and able to turn around content quickly, and escalated approval protocols (e.g., a single email address with all your approval stakeholders, including Corporate Communications, Legal, Regulatory, etc.).

If you believe your insights from market research or episodic, less frequent social listening efforts are sufficient, then that's a judgment call for you to make. However, I would argue that trends are taking shape and changing course faster today than ever before. Consider the rise of TikTok, which went from relative obscurity to the favored social media app for young users in less than a year. Regular, ongoing listening is the best way to give yourself an early advantage as trends take shape.

Finally, if you still think ideas born from social listening can't scale, consider the Toyota Sienna.

As recently as 2019, you could go to Toyota.com and find this staple of the minivan category presented as "the swagger wagon."

I first learned about the swagger wagon in 2011 when I was speaking at an event being hosted by the Word of Mouth Marketing Association (WOMMA). It was there that Toyota's marketing team presented the case study of how the original concept was unearthed through regular social listening in the comment threads on their YouTube channel. Although everyone knew the stereotypical head-hanging shame that was represented by buying your first minivan, the brand was inspired when it discovered an enthusiastic Sienna driver posted, "My Sienna gives me my swagger back!" The below excerpt is taken from the brand's award submission for an Effie award:

> Continued listening to our target paid off...The term "swagger wagon," mentioned in one of the YouTube videos, was being

bandied about on Twitter, Facebook, and YouTube. Suddenly, over forty "Swagger Wagon" fan pages appeared with the writers loving the term and all that it implied.

Toyota picked up on the comment and hired Hollywood director Jody Hill to make a spoof music video for the newly dubbed Swagger Wagon. The music video featured two parents rapping their minivan lifestyle, with a funky, hip-hop feel. It includes a litany of hilarious puns and relatable moments for parents while also promoting the minivan. After scenes of cereal spills and nurse mom healing boo-boos, Dad's mic drop line is, "We rock the S.E. not an SUV, and it's true if I were you, I'd be jealous of me."

Source: SWAGGER WAGON Official Toyota Music Video HD.

Here's the amazing thing. It wasn't just that Swagger Wagon surpassed 18 million views on YouTube. The brand also received over $1 billion worth of unpaid media impressions and surpassed its goal of selling 80,000 minivans in nine months. In fact, somewhat unbelievably, the Swagger Wagon remained the Toyota Sienna's brand for more than ten years. If you visited Toyota.

com, you wouldn't just be shown that famous featured video. The brand's entire creative approach shifted because of this one nugget from social listening, such that the Toyota Sienna *was* the Swagger Wagon.

Let's consider this case study in the context of the four common objections mentioned previously. The Sienna team no doubt had plenty of market research about their consumer. However, they still had the commitment to actively listen to customers commenting on their social media pages. Then they identified the signal in the noise and redeployed marketing resources to produce a big-budget music video. Once it was clear this campaign was a success, they pivoted their whole marketing strategy to embrace the Swagger Wagon at scale.

Ten years later, in the comments section of this video on YouTube, you'll notice at least one woman who saw the ad as a teenager and has since married, had kids, and bought her Sienna: at least for her, the video hit on certain emotional truths about the transition into adulthood. Just because she had kids and a minivan didn't mean she had lost her swagger. In fact, maybe her Swagger Wagon helped her get it back.

Consumers today expect you to listen to them. And they reward you when you do. You may not be able to turn new products around within two weeks, but you can be on-trend with your communications and marketing messages. You just have to listen to your audience and pick up the messages they're leaving for you.

SUBSTANTIATING WITH EVIDENCE

Since the dawn of time, companies and people have used hyperbolized claims to sell products. In fact, the Food and Drug

Administration and later the Federal Trade Commission were both created in large part as a response to companies using fake science to mislead the public. In the late 1800s and early 1900s, "patent medicines" were marketed as remedies for everything from colic in babies to cancer in grown-ups. Upon inspection, the products turned out to contain mostly alcohol and opiates, thus prompting the government to intervene.

Today, the incentive to use science that sells remains as strong as ever. Eighty-nine percent of people surveyed for the *Friction Fatigue Report* said they would be more likely to buy a product that was supported by scientific evidence. However, the investment required for meaningful evidence has led many brands to shy away. In fact, looking at editorial news over the past thirty years, there is a marked decline in the prevalence of both scientific studies being cited and experts being quoted. According to data from Newspaper.com, not only has the total number of experts and research studies being cited plummeted since 1990, but it has also done so at a greater rate relative to all instances of people being mentioned or quoted. The starkest drop-off occurred in the early 2000s when Google started draining resources from news outlets.

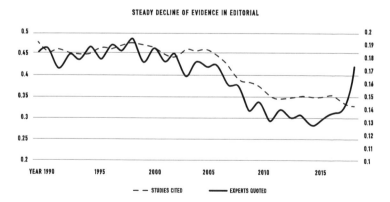

STEADY DECLINE OF EVIDENCE IN EDITORIAL

Source: Newspapers.com

The obvious exception appears with a huge upswing in experts being quoted in the last few years. This can largely be attributed to consumer and editorial backlash against "fake news" and "alternative facts."

One of the places this trend toward less rigorous marketing claims is most obvious is in the grocery store. The next time you're in the produce section, pay attention to how the food you're buying is marketed—specifically, the way the food contents themselves are described. For years, food products have been subject to stringent claims criteria by the FTC (thus "buttered popcorn" became "popcorn with butter-flavored topping"). However, recent trends in consumer preferences for things such as organic, natural, local, and artisanal products have created a gray area where these loosely defined terms can be interpreted any number of ways.

Nowhere is this more absurd than in the produce section, where you can now see things such as, "Tomatoes...*from the vine*." Honestly, where else do you get tomatoes? In a similar way, things like "*from farm to kitchen*" have started popping up. Would anyone argue this accurately describes the produce supply chain? I guess it sounds better than saying, *from farm to refrigerated truck to grocery store to kitchen*, but that doesn't mean you should turn it into a marketing claim. My personal favorite is when produce like fruit or vegetables are labeled as *artisanal*. I worked two summers on a farm while I was growing up in Iowa, and I can say with certainty that none of the farmers viewed themselves as corn or soybean artists.

That being said, these trends exist because they work. In particular, the millennial generation has embraced the idea of buying from smaller companies that claim to offer healthier options and are regionally close to them. In fact, one of my favorite insights into consumer behavior comes from charting the growth of organic food with the growth of Botox Cosmetic.

The two lines are almost perfectly collinear during the 2010s. Botox and organic food both boomed during this decade of consumers investing in premium products and prioritizing their health and appearance. However, when you ask this group of consumers WHY they choose organic food over non-organic food, the number one response they choose is...wait for it...*To avoid putting toxins in my body.* This answer is chosen more often than protecting the environment, preferring the taste, or believing them to be more nutritious.

Of course, many of these same consumers see no issue with injecting Botox (a neurotoxin) into their face. In fact, in a 2021 research report, more than half of organic produce consumers said they would consider getting Botox injections. This is a great incongruency in stated versus observed behavior, which always means a powerful truth is lurking. This truth is, unlike the more serious-minded Gen Z, the millennial generation does value status over substance, and empty marketing claims like *farm to kitchen* and *artisanal* produce convey a feeling of status.

But here's the rub: like all good consumer trends, the pendulum has already started swinging back. Ingredient lists are being dissected on Reddit, unsubstantiated claims are being called out on social media, and companies that say one thing but do another are being boycotted. The era of fake news, anti-vaxxers, climate deniers, and alternative facts created a healthy (or unhealthy) amount of skepticism among the general public. They are expressing new demand for scientific support, credentialing, and social proof with third-party organizations and experts. For brands that are not in a position to conduct a scientifically valid but expensive research program, let's look at these two primary methods of substantiating marketing claims: expert credentialing and social proof.

CREDENTIALING BY THIRD-PARTY ORGANIZATIONS AND EXPERTS

Credentialing a brand has always been one of the core reasons to work with a PR firm. Young PR pros are taught right out of school to identify key opinion leaders (KOLs), train them to stay on message, and secure opportunities for them to speak those messages through the media—either on broadcast shows or by being quoted in editorial coverage. Of course, celebrity endorsements have always served a similar purpose, and for brands that are able to earn editorial awards like the *Good Housekeeping* seal of approval, these credentials are proven sales drivers across any number of categories.

The sources that consumers trust for this credentialing have shifted over time; influencers are replacing celebrities, social media doctors are replacing primary care physicians, and digitally native media outlets are replacing *Good Housekeeping*, for instance. But the spirit of credentialing a brand through a third party is alive and well with modern consumers. In fact, a cursory examination of Google search trends reveals an important shift in consumer behavior away from deal seeking in favor of seeking expertise and quality.

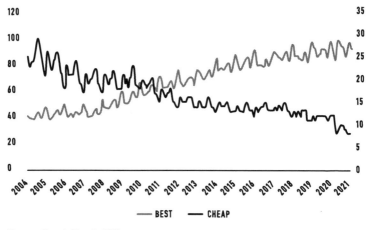

GOOGLE SEARCH TRENDS: BEST VS CHEAP

Source: Google Trends 2021.

Because being the "best" is itself a subjective term (whereas being "cheap" is relative but objective), it necessarily requires third-party validation. Somebody has to publish an article, ranking, or assessment of various choices in order to arrive at the best product.

In other words, reaching and persuading people who are seeking the "best" of anything requires substantiating your claims through third parties, including recognized experts and trustworthy media outlets. This truism becomes even more important when considering younger generations. In fact, from the *Friction Fatigue Report*, we discovered that young millennials and Gen Z are much more likely to be persuaded by third-party endorsement than older generations.

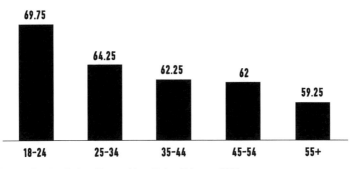

PERCENT WHO ARE MORE LIKELY TO TRUST A MARKETING CLAIM ABOUT A PRODUCT WHEN IT'S ENDORSED BY A THIRD PARTY

18-24	25-34	35-44	45-54	55+
69.75	64.25	62.25	62	59.25

Source: Friction Fatigue Report, Lippe Taylor, February 2021.

In 2019, at Lippe Taylor we partnered with a startup called Memo to conduct a research project into the elements of earned media that drive the greatest engagement and read time from consumers. We were specifically analyzing news articles published by top news outlets on their websites, and through our partnership with Memo we had access to the publisher's internal data about how many people were reading the articles and how engaged they were (did they scroll while reading, for example). One of the most important findings from our work with Memo sounds intuitive with our newfound awareness of psychological reactance. This finding is that, when considering news articles about products or brands in particular, those with a neutral tone greatly outperformed those with a positive or very positive tone. This finding was even more pronounced in articles that provided product reviews. In other words, when an article appears to be overly biased, people are likely to click away in a matter of seconds, whereas they're likely to spend more time reading articles that appear more measured.

COMPARISON OF ENGAGED TIMES
ACROSS ARTICLE TONES

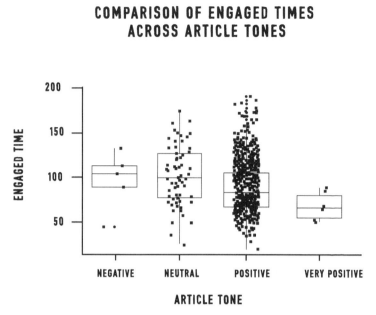

Source: Lippe Taylor peer-reviewed research with Memo.co data debuted at IPRRC 2020.

This insight makes sense intuitively, especially to marketers who pay attention to online reviews. We're going to talk more about reviews in the next section, but the responses and comment threads for reviews are often flush with people praising the neutral or balanced reviews while quietly ignoring the polarized ones. In fact, in a study titled "When Moderation Fosters Persuasion: The Persuasive Power of Deviatory Reviews," researchers at Boston University proved that "deviatory" reviews—those that deviate from the polarized positive/negative reviews—are seen as the most persuasive.[37]

In our *Friction Fatigue Report*, we found the same behavior applied to editorial news articles, with consumers ranking a balanced arti-

---

37 Daniela Kupor and Zakary Tormala, "When Moderation Fosters Persuasion: The Persuasive Power of Deviatory Reviews," *Journal of Consumer Research* 45, no. 3 (2018): 490–510, https://academic.oup.com/jcr/article-abstract/45/3/490/4938013?redirectedFrom=fulltext.

cle that included pros and cons of multiple products as being the
most influential over their purchase decisions. This phenomenon
was most exaggerated among older millennials (often termed
Xennials), less so among Gen Z, Gen X, and boomers.

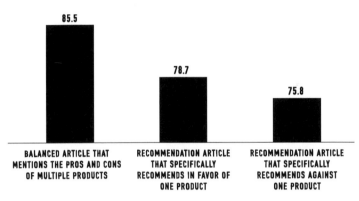

**WHICH OF THE FOLLOWING TYPE OF EDITORIAL ARTICLE
ABOUT A PRODUCT WOULD BE MOST LIKELY TO INFLUENCE
YOUR DECISION TO BUY THAT PRODUCT?**

85.5

78.7

75.8

| BALANCED ARTICLE THAT MENTIONS THE PROS AND CONS OF MULTIPLE PRODUCTS | RECOMMENDATION ARTICLE THAT SPECIFICALLY RECOMMENDS IN FAVOR OF ONE PRODUCT | RECOMMENDATION ARTICLE THAT SPECIFICALLY RECOMMENDS AGAINST ONE PRODUCT |

Source: Friction Fatigue Report, Lippe Taylor, February 2021

Although this makes intuitive sense on some level, most marketers shrug their shoulders when considering "balanced" or
"neutral" articles about their brand while celebrating articles
that offer a glowing endorsement. In fact, at Lippe Taylor, it's
common to see client emails exclaiming, "That article was like an
advertisement!" It's hard to resist the allure of emphatic endorsement from an editorial third party. And I'm not trying to dissuade
anyone from being excited.

There are two main takeaways from this research. First, don't
worry when a neutral and balanced article talks about your brand
in the context of competitors. It's probably working harder for
you than you realize. Second, once you've secured a stunning

editorial endorsement that reads like an advertisement, NOW is the time to go ahead and advertise.

One of the great innovations at Lippe Taylor was to be the first agency to introduce an Earned-to-Paid endorsement capability that allows brands to scale these rave editorial endorsements through paid media. In fact, the first time we approached a media outlet about this kind of program, they'd never heard of it and had no idea how to package it. The approach, which we call The Big E Engine® has since become relatively common practice at leading PR firms. It essentially means taking a great quote or headline from a news article, licensing the rights to use the media outlet's logo and imagery, and creating digital and paid social ads from it. The first time we tested this approach, the click-through rate on that brand's paid social ads quadrupled. Rather than promoting a self-serving marketing message, we were promoting what someone else had said about the brand—in this case, a dazzling endorsement from Refinery29 for the acne product Differin.

In 2017, leading dermatology company Galderma was launching its flagship prescription acne product, Differin, over the counter. Taking prescription medicines over the counter (what's known as the Rx-to-OTC switch) is notoriously difficult because insurance is no longer paying once the product sits on drugstore shelves instead of behind the pharmacy counter. Therefore, consumers need to be convinced to spend more for the product than before (a $10 copay might turn into a $15 or $20 product purchase), while the manufacturer is receiving dramatically less per product sold (a prescription product might cost $300 with insurance covering $290). To further complicate matters, the OTC acne category had been dominated by Johnson & Johnson for years and they would undoubtedly have larger advertising budgets and premium shelf space at retail for the foreseeable future.

Lippe Taylor led the launch of Differin when their advertising wasn't able to go live in time. The plan focused almost exclusively on third-party endorsement, credentialing, and substantiating the brand's claim that Differin was going to be a game changer for the acne category. Within the first year, we secured endorsements from 128 dermatologists, 72 influencers, 1,500 Amazon reviewers, and 10 editorial award programs (including Allure's Best of Beauty), along with hundreds of editorial news stories all substantiating our claims that Differin was a game changer. Within ten months, Differin reached the number one SKU in the acne category.

SOCIAL PROOF

Another one of the core reasons brands will often hire PR firms is to "normalize" something—that is, to make it seem like something that is novel, distinct, or deviant is in fact common. For the past eight years, Lippe Taylor has played an enormous role in normalizing Botox Cosmetic, which has evolved from being a hush-hush wrinkle eraser that celebrities would publicly swear off, to being so common in parts of the country that backyard barbecues include conversation about "Who does your Botox?" without even bothering to ask whether you're receiving the injections or not.

A large part of this evolution was due to social proof. Once it seemed like everyone else was using Botox Cosmetic, it became okay for, well, everyone else to do it. Richard Shotton, founder of Astroten Consultancy and the author of *Choice Factory*, is a leading expert in applying behavioral science to marketing. As part of our Lippe Taylor speaker series, he illustrated social proof by playing a clip from the classic television series *Candid Camera*. In the clip, one unsuspecting person enters an elevator with a group of people who are all paid actors. During the short elevator ride, the actors all suddenly turn to face the back wall, rather than the door of the elevator. The pressure to follow suit is palpable as the camera zooms into the confused person's face. However, the pressure to conform wins out and the person strangely turns around and stares into the back wall as if expecting something to happen.

If this sounds a lot like peer pressure, it is. However, social proof can be more than that. For years, social proof was a powerful tool used in advertising—think classic lines such as *the breakfast of champions* which features winning athletes who supposedly eat Wheaties, and *four out of five dentists recommend Trident*, which leverages both social proof and expert credentialing. There are also classic tactics of public relations firms that leverage social proof—things like pitching celebrities to the media so they can attest to using a product and publicizing photographs of them carrying a product on the street through tabloids.

The advent of social media, however, put jet fuel on the timeless behavioral truth that we are influenced by what other people (in particular popular people) are doing. With social media, we are being exposed to an idealized and curated presentation those people put forth. This fuels our desire to mimic their gram-worthy lifestyle in our own lives. There are three primary ways that marketers have taken advantage of this explosion in social proof: consumer reviews, user-generated content (UGC), and influencer marketing.

CONSUMER REVIEWS

In many ways, online product reviews represent the essence of social media for brands. For brands that are listening and responding, reviews offer both immediate feedback or market research, as well as opportunities to publicly make a good impression. For consumers, they represent the ultimate social proof. Rather than just asking one friend what they think, consumers can easily consult the opinions of hundreds. In fact, 93 percent of consumers say that online reviews have influenced their purchase decisions,[38] and 91 percent of eighteen- to thirty-four-year-olds trust online reviews as much as personal recommendations.[39]

Brett Hurt is a serial entrepreneur perhaps best known for having founded and served as CEO of Bazaarvoice from inception through its IPO. Bazaarvoice, which gets its name from being "the voice of the market" (get it—the voice of the bazaar?), became the de facto provider for online review technology during the 2010s. When Hurt launched the company, just three retailers provided the opportunity to review products on their websites. By the time he exited, they numbered in the thousands with nearly every major retailer and manufacturer using Bazaarvoice technology to power the review sections of their websites and consolidate their reviews across retailers.

Speaking to *CBS News*, Hurt reinforced not only the importance of social proof but also the collective wisdom of crowds when considering online reviews. "You can feel more confident about a product that has 200 reviews than one that has two reviews," he said. "As a consumer, you should look for at least five." Hurt then goes on to explain that consumer reviews follow a natural J curve with 4.3 stars being the natural resting place out of a possible 5.[40]

---

38   "Consumers Get 'Buy' with a Little Help from Their Friends," http://learn.podium.com/rs/841-BRM-380/images/2017-SOOR-Infographic.jpg.

39   Rosie Murphy, "Local Consumer Review Survey 2020," Bright Local, December 9, 2020, https://www.brightlocal.com/learn/local-consumer-review-survey/.

40   Sarah Butler, "How to Find the Useful Info in Online Customer Reviews," CBS News, August 11, 2011, https://www.cbsnews.com/news/how-to-find-the-useful-info-in-online-customer-reviews/.

The J-shaped distribution exists because consumers tend to be more motivated to post about very positive and very negative experiences—thus overemphasizing the occurrence of one-star and five-star reviews. Although the average product experience is more likely to belong in the two- through four-star range, those people are less motivated to post reviews about their experiences.

In fact, this phenomenon has been studied and proven true across billions of consumer reviews by Bazaarvoice, as well as through academic research. Researchers studying J curves in online reviews created a fake online review site where people were asked to rate a music CD, then compared their fake environment (in which every participant had to post a review) with the real-world Amazon reviews of the same CD. In the experiment, when every consumer was forced to post a review, a natural distribution of reviews presented like a bell curve:

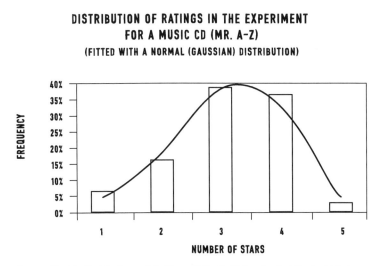

DISTRIBUTION OF RATINGS IN THE EXPERIMENT FOR A MUSIC CD (MR. A-Z)
(FITTED WITH A NORMAL (GAUSSIAN) DISTRIBUTION)

Source: Nan Hu, Paul Paviou, and Jie Zhang, "Why Do Online Product Reviews Have a J-Shaped Distribution?"

However, in the real world, where only very happy or very unhappy consumers take time to post their feedback, the distribution of online reviews for the same music CD displayed the polarized J curve:

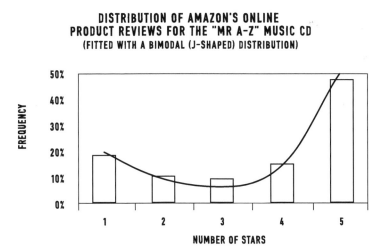

DISTRIBUTION OF AMAZON'S ONLINE PRODUCT REVIEWS FOR THE "MR A-Z" MUSIC CD
(FITTED WITH A BIMODAL (J-SHAPED) DISTRIBUTION)

Source: Nan Hu, Paul Paviou, and Jie Zhang, "Why Do Online Product Reviews Have a J-Shaped Distribution?"

This J curve is important for marketers for two reasons. First, it is a reminder that those people who did submit reviews do want to hear from you. They are the minority who were passionate enough to post about their experience—positive or negative—and their words are shaping how people feel about your product. Responding to them publicly is an important part of a sound social media strategy.

The second important takeaway from the J curve is that online reviews are not representative of the experience most people are having with a brand or product. In fact, most people are somewhere in the middle trough. This middle trough can be a dangerous place for a brand, though.

Michael Sabbia has moved on from Old Spice and is now the Senior Director of Marketing and Innovation at Galderma. He likens the trough of consumer experience to something called the warm tea trap. "Half of the world drinks hot tea," he explains. "And the other half drinks cold tea. So what big brands tend to do is to say, you know what would be great? We'll make warm tea. It's not hot, it's not cold, so it'll be perfect. Everyone will *kind of* like it." He goes on to explain the success of Old Spice was because they avoided the warm tea trap. "We were definitely not about warm tea. We decided that we were going to be cold tea. And if you liked hot and you thought cold tea sucked? Great. Don't drink it."

Sabbia has a point here. Three-star brands are in many ways the opposite of cult brands. Where cult brands engender intense enthusiasm from a niche audience, three-star brands are products that consumers just sort of buy because they're available. In a world dominated by traditional retail, there was plenty of room for three-star brands. Consumers would grab a household essential as they passed by in the drugstore aisle. However, today there is real danger in being a three-star brand. This passionless dead zone means you're a sitting duck for disruption. Not only does it mean consumers are likely to jump to a new brand that offers them something more exciting, the opposite is also true. Retailers are likely to target your three-star brand with a private label offering. If your brand isn't bringing consumers into a store, they might as well replace it with a product with a stronger contribution margin. Therefore, the main takeaway is that you should read your online reviews carefully, and if you're NOT getting a lot of polarized online reviews, you should reconsider whether your marketing efforts are amounting to warm tea.

USER-GENERATED CONTENT

UGC is, at least on the surface, what social media is all about. Regular people post updates and photos or videos about their days, their lives, and their opinions. Marketers engage by issuing a challenge, competition, or call for content that inspires people to talk about a brand or product in their social media posts. In many cases, the marketers may solicit rights to the content during or after the campaign so they can use it more widely in their marketing efforts. Perhaps the best example of this was Apple's Shot on iPhone campaign, which leverages photos taken by iPhone users around the world to show the power of the iPhone's camera.

UGC campaigns peaked in popularity in the early 2010s when social media users were still smitten by brands showing interest in their content. At that time, contests like Ritz Crackers' sweepstakes for photos that depicted recipes made with Ritz became so popular that social media users started to tire of participating. In fact, until the rise of TikTok, it appeared that UGC was all but dead for marketers. TikTok has put UGC back on the map with hashtag challenges like beauty brand e.l.f.'s #eyeslipsface challenge, which in 2020 prompted over five million TikTok users to post user-generated videos. Elsewhere, however, the influencer marketing boom has turned every consumer with a smartphone into a budding influencer, and consumers now wanted to be paid for their UGC. Even regular people with hundreds of followers have started branding themselves as "nano" influencers to follow in the footsteps of the "micro" influencers with low thousands of followers, and seemingly everybody wants to be paid to post about brands. For the right brands and the right campaigns, UGC is a great opportunity for brand marketers. However, the list of brands and creative campaigns that people will engage with for free is dwindling. For everyone else, there is influencer marketing.

INFLUENCER MARKETING

I've mentioned influencer marketing many times throughout this book, largely because it is one of the most prominent new vehicles for marketing messages. That is not, of course, to say that influencer marketing is "new" in any way. Rather, the discipline of influencer marketing has reached a new level of professionalism, scale, and importance to marketers who were already grappling with moving the resources from print and television into digital marketing channels.

As an early social media marketer, I've had a unique perspective on the growth and evolution of influencer marketing. Dating back to 2007 and 2008, I was working with influencers on MySpace and Digg.com, an often forgotten social media site that once sat on the top 100 list of all websites globally. As those sites faded, so did their influencers, but at every turn, there was a new wave of channels followed by influencers who were uniquely capable of reaching people on them. Twitter, Vine, Google Plus, and the Blogosphere all created platforms for people who rose from obscurity to reaching millions of social media users and commanding six- or seven-figure deals from brand marketers.

This latest influencer cycle is undoubtedly the first that has a feeling of permanence about it, largely because Gen Z and young millennials have embraced influencers with a sense of generational pride that's reminiscent of how older millennials (Xennials) embraced social media. In each of these examples (Gen Z with influencers and Xennials with social media), there was a feeling of exclusivity and belonging because it was your peers who had somehow managed to command respect and prominence at a young age. At Lippe Taylor, we've built a sizable business and specialist team dedicated entirely to influencer marketing. As part of this, we've developed a number of tools and frameworks for how to ensure clients are getting maximum value from their influencer partnerships, not least of which starts with identifying the right influencers who connect with the right motivation for a brand. Despite the near-constant evolution of the discipline, there are relatively common and consistent motivations behind why consumers follow influencers, regardless of what channel they're on. We capture these in our wheel of influence, which uses popular celebrity figures as archetypes to avoid the trap of picking an of-the-moment influencer who may not be the right partner.

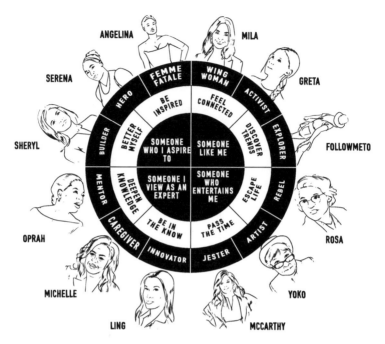

Source: StarlingAI (TM) Influencer Wheel, Lippe Taylor

This is not to say that influencer marketing such as we've seen it for the last few years isn't going to change, however. In 2018, I gave a keynote speech at Social Media Week in which I forecasted that influencer marketing of the sort that was currently in vogue was experiencing a hype cycle. That type of influencer marketing, in which brands hire primarily good-looking people to post heavily groomed photos and videos of their product fitting into a seemingly perfect life on Instagram and YouTube, was at the *peak of inflated expectations* phase of Gartner's hype cycle, and I cautioned marketers they should already be thinking about what's next.

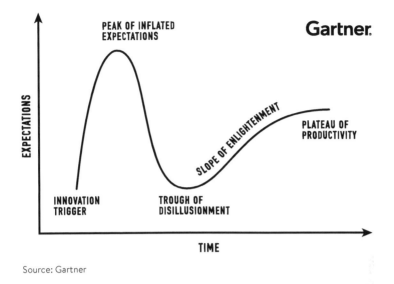

Source: Gartner

That prediction has proven true with the pandemic accentuating the *trough of disillusionment* in tone-deaf influencers who struggled to adapt as their followers endured a very different experience under lockdown. Even without the pandemic, trends were already underway, however, with the birth of TikTok creators showing how the pendulum does swing in exaggerated fashion. Where Instagram is overwhelmingly dominated by photoshopped and Facetuned models hocking products from idyllic locations, TikTok is the opposite. Top creators on TikTok are overwhelmingly regular people, dressed in regular clothes, posting goofy faces and unfiltered videos of themselves dancing and attempting silly "challenges" in their living rooms.

Whether you're the sort of brand that wants to be promoted by a perfectly filtered photo of a model or a goofy video of a teenager standing on her head is for you to determine. Either way, influencer marketing is forecast to be a $15 billion industry in

2022, up from $8 billion in 2019.[41] For young consumers, the most advertising-averse generations, influencers are one of the most preferred methods of discovering new products. But even aging and elderly consumers have found ways of becoming influencers these days. There's no doubt that sponsored influencer marketing is an important component in a modern marketing plan. However, as with any new and overhyped opportunity, there are also plenty of examples where brands have been taken advantage of. Influencers now have a whole cottage industry of managers, agents, producers, and promoters who exist to hype and sell them.

At Lippe Taylor, we've helped brands drive significant growth by partnering with the right influencers. The results have been as varied as the influencers themselves. In one instance, our influencer work helped a DTC brand acquire over 50,000 monthly paying customers at a 40 percent lower CAC (customer acquisition cost) than their existing benchmark. In another, we helped a heritage brand get distribution in Costco because the influencer campaign created an aura of hipness. In a third, we partnered with an influencer to co-create a whole new makeup line that sold out almost instantly.

We've also seen bad behavior and helped brands manage through what happens when influencer relationships go sour. One influencer tried blackmailing a brand with threats to falsely demonize their product, another demanded payment for content that clearly failed to meet the brief, and one broke her exclusivity clause by promoting competitor brands. One of the most publicized issues came when an influencer turned on the brand that had quite literally made her famous by publicly dumping the brand in the press after it didn't meet her exorbitant demands.

---

41   Insider Intelligence, "Influencer Marketing Report," Business Insider, January 6, 2021, https://www.businessinsider.com/influencer-marketing-report.

Perhaps most common, however, is influencers dramatically inflating their fee demands with tens of thousands of fake followers. All of these issues can cause both reputation concerns and general distractions for marketers who don't manage their influencer marketing programs properly.

Much like in the early days of social media, many brands look at influencer marketing and think it should be either turnkey enough to buy as a software service or intuitive enough to manage on their own. However, there are real risks to getting it wrong and a real opportunity for brands that get it right. I advise brands strongly against working with the turnkey influencer platforms. Anything that seems that easy—you simply enter your credit card, pick a few influencers, and watch the posts go live—is not going to deliver the kind of results you're imagining.

For brands that want to handle their own influencer marketing efforts internally, I advise they dedicate at least one person to it. If they're not able to make that level of commitment, then I recommend partnering with an agency that is on top of the ever-changing nuances from influencer identification to contracting, creative briefing, content production, promotion, and measurement. Much like buying a house, influencers have their own teams to represent their interests, and brands need to have the same.

BEING CULTURALLY RELEVANT

In 2013, the power went out in New Orleans. It was the middle of Super Bowl XLVII and Colin Kaepernick was anxiously pacing the field, eager to mount an attempted comeback against the Baltimore Ravens. The power outage lasted for thirty-four minutes—an eternity for players waiting to resume the game of their lives but a mere moment in the realm of producing marketing assets. In fact, for most content studios, thirty-four minutes isn't even enough time to talk about the purpose of a piece of content, let alone concept, produce, and distribute it. Yet, that is exactly what Oreo's social media newsroom team did. In that briefest of windows, the team from 360i put out a simple but of-the-moment image on Twitter that read, *You Can Still Dunk in the Dark*.

YOU CAN STILL DUNK IN THE DARK

Source: Oreo Cookie. Twitter Post. February 4, 2013.

It was artfully crafted—not specifically naming the Super Bowl (heaven forbid you draw the NFL's ire)—but clearly referencing a cultural moment that millions of people were witnessing.

The result was instant consumer kudos for the cookie brand, which had recently celebrated its 100th anniversary. More than 15,000 people retweeted the image on Twitter and over 20,000 liked it on Facebook. Perhaps most importantly, it spawned an earned media news cycle that would earn the simple post a place in marketing history.

Kate Charles, who is now Chief Planning Officer at Lippe Taylor, led the social listening team behind that tweet. "I have to admit, we had no idea this simple post would essentially be inducted to the marketing hall of fame someday and become synonymous with 'real-time marketing.' What we did know was everyone would be turning to their phones when the power went. We just wanted to acknowledge that we were going through the same thing, at the same time, as everyone else. It was our way of being culturally relevant."

Her sentiment was reinforced by Lisa Mann, who was VP of Cookie Marketing at Mondelez when the power went out. "Oreo is a real-time brand, a real-time marketer, and we are a part of our culture and the fabric of our community," Mann explained in a 2013 interview with *Forbes*.[42] "It is our objective to be as relevant today as we were 100 years ago when we launched."

Being "of culture," or more simply stated "culturally relevant," has become a common pursuit for brands today, and no wonder. According to the *Friction Fatigue Report*, 69.25 percent of people say they *expect* brands to be culturally relevant. However, what exactly that phrase means—cultural relevance—can differ based on the context. *Merriam-Webster* defines culture as *the customary beliefs, social forms, and material traits of a racial, religious, or social group*, and also, *the characteristic features of everyday existence shared by people in a place or time*. Therefore, it stands to reason that for brands to be culturally relevant, they need to demonstrate shared beliefs, social forms, and material traits with the audience they are trying to engage...in a common place or time.

---

42 Jenny Rooney, "Behind the Scenes of Oreo's Real-Time Super Bowl Slam Dunk," *Forbes*, February 4, 2013, https://www.forbes.com/sites/jenniferrooney/2013/02/04/behind-the-scenes-of-oreos-real-time-super-bowl-slam-dunk/?sh=40f0dfa62e66.

Let's look at these defining characteristics in reverse order, starting with shared material traits.

For many years, Red Bull has been viewed as an anomaly in brand marketing. Their ability to integrate the brand into subcultures such as extreme sports, e-gaming, and performative arts while being overtly branded seems to defy generally accepted trends about consumers disliking heavily branded marketing efforts. They even have popular professional sports teams that are simply named The Red Bulls.

What's important to note about Red Bull's approach is that for each subculture they engage with, they first earn their place among them. This is done through a marketing team that's entirely dedicated to culture (in fact, it's called the Culture Team). Members of this team specialize in subcultures and operate by hiring regionally located team members who are truly passionate about the sport or cultural passion point they are engaging in. These team members' job is to ensure the brand is engaging in the right grassroots activities and to demonstrate that Red Bull does share the same material traits that define a subculture—ramps for skate parks, stereo equipment for rap battles, wingsuits for extreme athletes, and the list goes on. When Red Bull wants to engage in a community, it doesn't just sponsor the top athletes (it does that, too); it shows up at the ground level. For context, let's contrast the brand's success in extreme sports to Microsoft's largely ineffective attempt at using professional football to drive adoption of its Surface tablet.

Rather than starting on the ground floor like Red Bull, right after Super Bowl XLVII became christened the Blackout Bowl, Microsoft inked a massive deal—reportedly worth $400 million, with the NFL as it tried to combat the cool factor and commercial success of Apple's iPad. The deal stipulated that all coaches and commentators for NFL games would be required to use Surface tablets. In most cases, the tablets would be replacing clipboards and handwriting tools rather than Apple iPads, and Microsoft hoped the cachet of the NFL would help its Surface tablet out-flank Apple.

The deal has been repeatedly characterized as an unmitigated catastrophe as commentators mistakenly referenced using their "iPad" on air, Chicago Bears quarterback Jay Cutler referred to the tablets as "knockoff iPads" on national television, and Aaron Rodgers was filmed smashing his Surface, which had apparently glitched, after throwing an interception. Chip Kelly, 49ers coach, said of the Surface in a broadcast interview that "sometimes it doesn't work and you have to shake it a little bit," before his star quarterback, Colin Kaepernick, weighed in by joking he had to hit the side of it whenever the screen froze. The jokes ended, though, when the New England Patriots loudly blamed their Microsoft Surface tablets after their loss in the AFC championship game. The truth is that Microsoft's tablets were not to blame—their tablets didn't connect because of a Wi-Fi issue. A poor Wi-Fi connection would have impacted Apple iPads just as much as Microsoft Surface tablets; however, the handwriting tools the coaches had previously used would have worked just fine.

Wi-Fi connection issues aside, why did Microsoft find itself in the crosshairs? On the one hand, it was a failure of change manage-ment—most of these players, coaches, and commentators were accustomed to using pen and paper. That speaks to the larger issue, though, which is that none of them ASKED for tablets. They were being forced to use them because of an advertising deal. Not only is this bad for psychological reactance, but it also relates to something called the personal affect bias. John Daly is a management professor in the McCombs School of Business at the University of Texas. He describes this phenomenon as simply, "When people like you, you can do no wrong. When they dislike you, you can do no right." Microsoft didn't put in the effort to be liked. Instead, they bought their way into every coach, player, and commentator's hands with an advertising deal, and they were resented for it.

According to Wikipedia, there are 6,376 high school football programs in America. What would have happened if Microsoft had started at the ground level and outfitted those programs with Surface tablets so that coaches and players grew up learning the game with Microsoft? Then maybe when Aaron Rodgers threw an interception, he would have looked elsewhere—blaming the play call, the sun in his eyes, maybe even the Wi-Fi, but not his Microsoft Surface tablet. That's what Red Bull would have done, and that's how Red Bull has used *shared material traits* to earn its place among the subcultures it engages with.

The second aspect of culture—shared social forms—takes on a literal interpretation for brands engaging in social media. Consumers are showing us every day how they engage and interact with their friends online. Is your brand engaging in the same places and the same ways?

Often, when marketers talk about culturally relevant marketing tactics, they are referring to a timely (or "real-time") marketing communication that happens while people are tuned into a trending topic or meme, or a popular moment in sports or entertainment. Similar to Oreo during the Super Bowl, the most common examples of this are brands commenting or posting about whatever is happening in their audience's feeds at the moment.

These days, people are less awestruck by brands posting immediate reactions to cultural moments. In fact, what earned Oreo's agency marketing stardom is now a simple expectation among consumers in some categories, such as snacking. This doesn't mean that opportunities for culturally relevant marketing have diminished, though. Quite the opposite, because consumers are conditioned to look for tried-and-true tactics like real-time tweeting, the reaction is all the greater when brands manage to surprise them. In fact, from the *Friction Fatigue Report*, we found that 75.65 percent of consumers say they like seeing brands engage in cultural moments.

More recently, in February 2020, Jif peanut butter demonstrated their cultural relevance—and their shared social form but partnering with Giphy to weigh in on the long-running cultural conversation about the proper pronunciation of the image file format gif.

Jif and its agencies even put out a limited-release peanut butter jar with both spellings on opposite sides of the container (JIF and GIF). The discussion then moved swiftly to Giphy, a popular website for meme culture, which generated more than 434 million views on Jif vs. Gif content. Finally, a fake linguist—Gary Goodman, PhD—was consulted to settle the debate, humorously using alternative pronunciations of words such as Gettysburg with a hard and soft *G*. The results? An 8.3 percent increase in Jif sales and $137 million in Earned Media value.

Depending on the seriousness of the cultural moment (athletes taking a knee during the national anthem is much more serious than the Super Bowl lights going out), simply commenting on something without contributing to the cause can be seen as derivative. And there's no doubt consumers are starting to frown upon brands promoting frivolous programs like the Jif vs. Gif debate when there are more serious topics in the world to consider.

This leads us to the third and final aspect of brands participating in culture—demonstrating shared beliefs. Often referred to as *cultural competency* in the context of DEI (diversity, equity, and inclusion) and a brand's efforts to communicate in an inclusive way, this aspect of marketing has evolved significantly in recent years. In particular, the calls for racial justice, national unity, and greater inclusivity reached a fever pitch in the wake of a national movement to protest police brutality in 2020.

We'll talk later about how brands can start or contribute to societal conversations. This is a nuanced and tricky needle to thread for many brands, and identifying the right conversation and the right tone for the brand should not be taken lightly. However, there's no doubt that today's most successful brands are abandoning their former milquetoast positions and taking a stronger stand on social issues.

In this area, Procter & Gamble aspires to be a leader among marketers. In April 2017, P&G's CFO, Jon Moeller, said in an earnings call the company was tasking its agencies with creating culture-defining advertisements. As a reminder, despite its popularity as one of the world's largest advertisers, P&G's actual business is making toilet paper, toothpaste, and deodorant (among other things). No doubt, Mr. Moeller writes more big checks to Big Advertising than anybody else in the world. However, the idea that company executives believed a toilet paper manufacturer had any kind of right to define culture illustrates how self-deluded the advertising industrial complex had become.

Rather than *defining* any aspect of culture, what P&G did do is produce lots of ads that *observed* aspects of culture—for instance, the Gillette commercial of an adult man helping his aging father shave, or the Herbal Essences commercial that encouraged women to embrace change while proclaiming, "Changing my hair changed my life," and perhaps most notably, the beautiful and highly acclaimed campaign "The Talk" that observed the difficult conversation Black parents have with their children about the disadvantages they face.

In all of these instances, P&G produced beautiful videos that observed an aspect of contemporary culture while hocking their brands. They did not actually define anything about that culture for two reasons. First, because they are a toilet paper manufacturer. Second, because they are advertisers, not activists. Advertisers seek to create relevance with the people they are selling to and P&G seeks to do this at scale. For P&G, this means making ads about something that millions of people can already relate to.

Not only do these ads lack anything that could be construed as controversial or more than mildly thought-provoking, but they also do a masterful job of avoiding the actual cultural conversation. Could "The Talk" have made a larger point about white privilege or supporting racial justice? Absolutely. But that would have been a gamble when you still need to sell toilet paper to millions of white people.

Contrast this with Nike. The brand was built almost entirely on the basis of its extraordinary deal with Michael Jordan. Nike knew who its customer was, and it also knew what role the brand needed to play. A few years before signing Jordan, when Nike was still a relatively fledgling apparel company, Phil Knight had announced at a shoe conference that he wasn't in the shoe business—he was in the *entertainment* business.

Years later, Jordan had an equally famous quote of his own when he asserted, "Republicans buy shoes, too," when advising athletes and sporting brands to steer clear of politics. However, in 2018, one year after Jon Moeller's bold statement about culture-defining ads at P&G, Nike rejected the advice that Jordan had given many years before. In doing so, the company conducted a masterclass in how brands can truly be culture-defining. Demonstrating the difference between an advertiser and an activist, Nike chose to partner with athlete and activist Colin Kaepernick to amplify his message rather than manufacturing one of their own.

That message, which Kaepernick had been promoting ever since taking the field as a backup quarterback and leading the 49ers all the way to Super Bowl XLVII in New Orleans, was to protest police brutality against Black Americans. Kaepernick pioneered the movement of athletes taking a knee during the national anthem as a form of protest and is widely believed to have been blacklisted by NFL team owners as a result. Kaepernick lost his position as an NFL quarterback for refusing to stand for the anthem. Nike seized the opportunity to amplify his activism with a simple message: *Believe in something, even if it means sacrificing everything*, the ad read.

Source: Kaepernick, Colin. Twitter Post. September 3, 2018.

The ad launched first on Kaepernick's personal social media pages and then moved to television. Nike had paid to run the spot at a time when the majority of white America and nearly all Republicans disagreed with players like Kaepernick kneeling for the national anthem. The conversation erupted online, with the now infamous image above being shared on every feed whether you agreed or disagreed with the sentiment.

It was a gamble for Nike; the campaign infuriated millions of people who were staunchly opposed to what Kaepernick stood (or kneeled) for. Michael Sabbia points to this campaign as the ultimate example of a brand rejecting the notion of warm tea: "You've got people who are burning shoes and throwing them away and Nike is saying, that's fine, we don't want those people anyway."

However, the gamble paid off. Despite the movement to boycott Nike, the company's market cap soared $6 billion. A year later, 35 percent of people supported athletes kneeling for the anthem, up from 28 percent in 2016. By mid-2020, according to a Yahoo! News/YouGov poll, that number was 52 percent.[43] Sabbia elaborates, "This is what it means to take a strong stance. The future is bright for Nike because young people now believe, THIS is my brand. It has been solidified as their brand versus one of many they might have considered beforehand." He's right about the long-term prospects for Nike. This is also what it means to define culture and very few brands have the platform, the credibility, or the guts to pull it off.

By contrast, P&G's sales, market share, and stock price all declined that same year. The main takeaway is that all the advertising in the world can't create cultural relevance if you're not able or willing to do something with cultural impact.

So what about those brands that don't have the prominence or the positioning to have larger cultural impact? Being culturally relevant is considered a necessity for brands today, but not every brand can sway the course of public opinion like Nike. For these

---

43   Jay Busbee, "Yahoo News/YouGov Poll: Majority of Americans Now Support NFL Players' Right to Protest," Yahoo!Sports, June 11, 2020, https://sports.yahoo.com/poll-majority-of-americans-now-support-nfl-players-right-to-protest-151212603.html.

brands, there is still a meaningful opportunity—sometimes even an expectation—to demonstrate the brand's contemporary relevance through either what's known as culture hacking or by amplifying a cultural conversation that's already taking place.

Identifying a brand's place in culture and demonstrating cultural relevance is perhaps one of the most difficult but rewarding endeavors available to marketers today. It all starts with listening to both branded and unbranded conversations to understand how people feel about your brand and what other topics matter to them. Once you've really heard your audience, it's time to start engaging with them.

ENGAGING WITH PEOPLE INDIVIDUALLY

In 2018, Samsung was one of the largest advertisers on Facebook, spending roughly $80 million on Facebook Ads for their mobile phone division alone. They also employed a team of young community managers to answer all the comments on the Samsung Facebook page. That team responded to 300,000 comments in a single year.

Today, it's widely accepted that community managers play a key role in "organic" or "always on" social media strategies. They're also often discussed in relation to customer service. But what's rarely discussed is how effective they can be at driving marketing results. In a sophisticated market mix modeling exercise, the $80 million spent on Facebook Ads was credited with 1.14 percent brand lift (Samsung's proxy measure for sales). By comparison, the 1:1 interactions by Samsung's community managers were found to be responsible for a 0.41 percent brand lift. I don't know exactly how much those community managers were paid, but they were a hell of a deal. Brand marketers should make space in their mental and resourcing models for engaging with customers in a 1:1 dialogue.

It's well understood this kind of personal interaction with customers is an important part of the DTC playbook. Brands like Dollar Shave Club, Glossier, Casper, and hundreds of others who have disrupted entrenched brands and disintermediated middlemen like retailers have demonstrated a strong commitment to engaging people directly in social media. Perhaps it comes more naturally when you're responsible for marketing a brand that was born on the internet as opposed to one that was built during the advertising era. Anne Talley, former Global Brand President at Revlon, describes this by saying, "Their disruption is coming from the ability of these brands to have a direct interaction with consumers that wasn't there in the past."

While heritage brands have labored over making their ads more millennial-friendly, DTC brands have rebalanced their marketing budgets to prioritize the kind of marketing these customers enjoy, rather than interruptive advertisements. And it's working. For several years now, these DTC brands have been kicking their entrenched competitors' butts (although with pandemic-motived nostalgia, heritage brands did regain a lot of ground).

This is not to say these DTC brands don't advertise—they do. But the advertising takes up a much smaller portion of their budget, while things such as product innovations, direct customer engagement, and partnering with influencers differentiate them.

One of the things preventing established companies from making larger commitments to direct customer engagement is that it's most often considered a cost center. These companies took the customer care model of answering calls to their 800 number and applied it to social media. Therefore, they tend to incentivize their customer service people to "close out" interactions with customers as quickly as possible, thus allowing them to respond to more complaints with quickfire, boilerplate answers. They're trying to spend as little time as possible with their customer because they think of them as only having complaints.

Meanwhile, DTC brands look at one-on-one engagement with consumers as marketing. The way these brands are operating feels more like this: "Every chance I have to make a good impression on someone, I'm taking it." Much like how media outlets are reshaping who they think of as being their customer (more as the audience, less as the advertiser), this simple redefinition of consumer engagement can reshape your approach and transform the outcome. This kind of commitment to personal interaction—to be further explored in Chapter 6—leads to a better purchase experience, happier customers, and better reviews. Brands like Glossier and CeraVe (see more in the Conclusion) stand out because of their direct consumer engagement: their campaigns succeeded largely without old-school advertising.

DOING MORE THAN SELLING A PRODUCT

The final expectation modern consumers have of brands is that they do more than selling a product. In fact, from the *Friction Fatigue Report*, we found that more than 72 percent of people believe that brands should "do more than just selling products." That number goes up a little bit for younger consumers. But by and large, it's the same among all demographics. The most obvious example of brands doing more is cause marketing—the idea that brands can "do well by doing good." According to 2020's CMO Survey, which is conducted every year by the Duke Fuqua School of Business, 79 percent of CMO's believe that customers are expressing "greater acknowledgment of companies' attempts to do good."[44]

However, there are many ways brands can meet the expectation of doing more than selling a product. I've condensed them here because it's rare that a brand can credibly accomplish more than one of them. The thing that's certain, though, is that brands that focus solely on promoting products are sitting ducks for disruption from brands that do more. Here are the four primary ways that brands that "do more" get rewarded by consumers today:

1. Experience Can Be Everything
2. Creating a Lifestyle Perception
3. Contributing to Societal Conversations
4. Embracing a Purposeful Mission

EXPERIENCE CAN BE EVERYTHING

Not surprisingly, when marketers take on new brand assignments, they often want to jump straight to the creative and big-picture work—things such as purpose marketing and building a lifestyle brand. Not only is this work inspiring personally, but when looking at the data, it also seems like the best way to connect with consumers. However, among the four ways brands can do more, the customer experience is the one with the most potential to hurt a brand if ignored. The other three are not without pitfalls, and it's true that inaction in some cases can work against a brand. But there are countless examples of successful brands that choose NOT to create lifestyle brands, engage in societal conversations, or embrace purposeful missions.

---

44 Duke's 2020 CMO Survey, https://cmosurvey.org/results/february-2020/ and https://cmosurvey.org/results/special-covid-19-edition-june-2020/.

On the other hand, brands that choose not to focus on perfecting the customer experience can very easily find their inaction is responsible for the brand's decline or disruption. Perhaps that is why in the 2021 version of Duke's CMO Survey, 33 percent of CMOs rated "strong customer experience" as their number one priority—placing it ahead of product quality, innovation, pricing, and service.[45] In other words, the first imperative for marketers is to make sure their house is in order with customer experience.

Customer experience can be a complicated and wide-ranging topic, which also relates to other key concepts from this chapter, such as listening to your customers and engaging with them in a 1:1 dialogue. It can also relate to big-picture, creative brand experiences like we'll see with the Taco Bell Hotel in a few pages. First things first, however, it means sitting down and taking a painstakingly deliberate walk through how people are experiencing your brand.

In 2018, PwC issued a landmark report titled *Experience Is Everything: How to Get It Right*. To conduct the report, PwC surveyed 15,000 people around the world, 4,000 of whom were in the United States.[46] They reported several important findings that may sound intuitive but with an emphasis that goes far beyond the level most brands place on it. In fact, through PwC's annual Digital IQ study, they found that the number of companies that say creating better customer experiences is a digital priority dropped to 10 percent in 2017, down from 25 percent in 2016.

According to PwC, the opportunities for brands that do focus

---

45   Duke's 2021 CMO Survey, https://cmosurvey.org/wp-content/uploads/2021/02/The_CMO_Survey-Highlights_and_Insights_Report-February-2021.pdf.

46   "Experience Is Everything," PwC, https://www.pwc.com/us/en/services/consulting/library/consumer-intelligence-series/future-of-customer-experience.html.

here include improved marketing outcomes, premium pricing, and increased loyalty. Specifically, 65 percent of respondents said a positive experience with a brand is more influential than great advertising (never mind mediocre or bad advertising). And depending on the product category, consumers will spend up to 16 percent more for products that offer a good experience, while 32 percent of consumers will walk away from a brand they love after one bad experience.

The fundamentals of a positive experience are simple and straightforward: convenient, friendly service, easy transactions, a trustworthy brand, and human interaction. I strongly recommend every brand marketer experiences every aspect of their brand as a consumer would and does so frequently. You should also ask people in your life who are notoriously cynical, pessimistic, and judgmental to do the same thing. Doing so will go further in helping you get your house in order than paying for another customer journey map. Once your house is in order with the fundamentals, the next order of experience drivers are where marketers get to have a lot of fun. These include things such as providing unique experiences, enhancing the brand image, and creating an atmosphere of fun for the brand. One of the best such examples came courtesy of none other than Taco Bell.

In 2019, Taco Bell launched a pop-up experience in Palm Springs, which was aptly titled the Taco Bell Hotel. This weekend renovation of The V hotel in Palm Springs brought together the best of The Bell as a sort of special edition getaway for its biggest fans. From Taco Bell breakfast in bed to the poolside Baja Bar and the Freeze Lounge, guests were treated to the best food and flavor the brand had to offer. At the salon, you could pick your favorite braids and add a sauce packet flower for $10.

Not only did the Taco Bell Hotel come as a surprising move from a fast food chain, but it also served to dazzle superfans, food writers, influencers, and brand ambassadors with first takes on new menu items, which launched nationally shortly thereafter. Taco Bell was able to do this because its house was already in order. Consumers were emphatic about expressing their love for the brand. Once the fundamentals are in place, consumers today want to **experience** brands rather than just purchasing them. Great brands provide them with memorable experiences whether that's in a store, in their shopping cart, with the chat box, on social media, via the phone, or while checking into their Taco Bell Hotel poolside suite. The exclusivity of the Taco Bell Hotel gave it the allure of special edition releases and the ability to brag on Instagram about your insider experience.

Recent academic research points to the behavioral preference for unique experiences. In a report on the consumption of collectable experiences,[47] researchers from Harvard and Columbia Universities sought to address the questions, "Why on earth do people stay in ice hotels?" and "Why do they eat bacon-flavored ice cream?" They found that collecting unusual experiences gives consumers a feeling of productivity even during their leisure time. They went on to describe the modern pursuit of developing an "experiential CV"—in other words, a person's résumé of collected experiences, as a reaction to the deluge of luxury goods available today. When there are so many high-end products available, collecting them no longer provides the same level of self-fulfillment or advancement. On the other hand, collecting a penthouse stay at the Taco Bell Hotel is most certainly worth putting on the experiential CV.

---

47 Anat Keinan and Ran Kivetz, "Productivity Mindset and the Consumption of Collectable Experiences", *NA—Advances in Consumer Research*, vol 35 (2008): 101-105. https://www.acrwebsite.org/volumes/13286/volumes/v35/NA-35.

It's important to note the Taco Bell Hotel was the culmination of many years spent experimenting with experiential marketing. The brand has created dozens of pop-up experiences and even opened a Taco Bell restaurant inside a Las Vegas chapel, where more than 200 couples have been married and eaten Taco Bell in the same place.

Perhaps one of the greatest lessons from the Taco Bell Hotel is that consumers may hate advertising, but that doesn't mean they hate marketing. The Taco Bell Hotel was literally dripping in branded marketing messages—with pool floats, throw pillows, bed scarfs, wall hangings, and even wallpaper being branded Taco Bell. In fact, staying at the ultra-branded hotel wasn't even free. Consumers had to shell out normal hotel room prices in order to stay there. The difference is that Taco Bell created a fun and engaging experience and allowed consumers to enjoy it on their own terms.

Taco Bell is not the only brand investing in this kind of marketing experience. Explaining how he transformed marketing at Master-card, Raja Rajamannar says, "What I have done is move money from traditional advertising—a lot of it—into experiences…I keep telling them advertising is dead. Advertising is all about story-telling—so I say storytelling is dead. The future is storymaking. If I have to fast forward ten years, the marketing and advertis-ing mix is going to be completely different. Experiences will be predominant."

Creativity will always be at the heart of marketing that consumers enjoy, which is why the advertising industry's defiant claim to being the "creative industry" was an industry-wide masterstroke. Whether it takes the form of inspiration, beauty, thoughtfulness, or humor, consumers like being entertained and engaged by brands. The problem is, the vast majority of advertising does not meet the standard where consumers would willingly engage with it. That's why media plans instead focus so much effort on interrupting them. But forcing people to watch an ad they would otherwise skip was always a failing strategy. Now that consumers have been exposed to so much brilliant creativity from brands that do more than just sell products, they are primed to judge your advertisement even more harshly.

CREATING A LIFESTYLE PERCEPTION

"Consumers pay one dollar for a sixteen-ounce can of Monster and two dollars for an eight-ounce can of Red Bull," then-Chief Digital Officer at Red Bull Media House Lukas Cudrigh told me. He finished by saying, "The difference in that dollar is the Red Bull lifestyle."

That halo effect—the perception that Red Bull represents not a canned beverage but a lifestyle—was hard earned. The brand made a conscious decision to prioritize its marketing investments in what's known as a brand-as-publisher model. Meaning that instead of spending all of its marketing dollars with publishers, Red Bull decided to BECOME one. Thus, things like Red Bull TV, Red Bull Originals (documentary films), and the *Red Bulletin* (a print magazine) all made strategic sense as the company built a media brand to complement its beverage brand. Many brands have embraced the brand-as-publisher model over the years, but few, if any, have remained so committed to it.

One of the most unique investments the company has made into the Red Bull lifestyle, however, is the company's creation of specialized sporting events. Not only has Red Bull sponsored extreme sports athletes for decades, but it has also invented entire sporting events such as Air Race, Crashed Ice, and Flug-tag to create an almost Rube Goldberg-like sense of adventurous competition where none existed before. In addition to these brand creations, Red Bull has also been uniquely committed to rooting out and supporting underground passion areas such as breakdancing and e-sports (competitive video gaming) long before they were on the national radar.

In all of these marketing efforts, the Red Bull logo is plastered on every visible surface, but nobody cares that they're being marketed to. Red Bull made this experience possible—how could they feel anything but excitement for a brand like that?

Another important and instructive aspect of Red Bull's success is that like the skateboarding and mountain biking athletes they sponsor, the Red Bull lifestyle is "all or nothing." As Lukas Cudrigh explained to me, "You'll never find Red Bull giving a discount. We give the cans away at every event and charge full price in stores. It's *full price or free*."

This philosophy of full price or free fits with consumer behavior. People feel good when they make an expensive or full-priced purchase for themselves. And they feel special when they are given something valuable for free. The pervading wisdom that couponing and discounts should be part of growing CPG brands was born in the days when retailers were the customer. Retailers like coupons because they bring people into retail stores. The actual appeal of discounts to consumers is far less than the appeal of getting something for free, though. In the popular psychology bestseller *Predictably Irrational*, author Daniel Ariely uses a simple experiment to demonstrate. When given the choice of spending $0.26 for a premium Lindt chocolate or $0.01 for a lower quality Hershey's Kiss, 73 percent of consumers choose

Lindt. However, decrease the cost by one penny, such that Lindt's chocolate is $0.25 and the Hershey's Kiss is free, and the behavior flips. Sixty-nine percent choose the Hershey's Kiss.

Source: Dan Ariely, *Predictably Irrational* (New York: HarperCollins, 2008); image credit to SBO Financial.

Writing for *Psychology Today*, PhD Psychologist Eva Krockow explains this phenomenon in two ways: First, people experience a positive emotional feeling when receiving an unexpected gift, and second, their expectations are lower and therefore easily surpassed when they've received something for free.[48] Regardless of the specific mechanism, it's clear that free products engender a powerful emotional response in consumers. For Red Bull, the expectation that free cans will accompany every Red Bull event also helps drive turnout, thus fueling a self-fulfilling cycle of brand love. Come to Red Bull's events and you'll have a great experience.

---

48   Eva M. Krockow, "Why We Love Free Stuff Too Much," *Psychology Today*, August 8, 2019, https://www.psychologytoday.com/intl/blog/stretching-theory/201908/why-we-love-free-stuff-too-much.

There are of course other brands that have also done an extraordinary job of creating a lifestyle perception. Jeep is a great example, where owners seem to believe they all belong to a club simply for having bought the same car. In recent years, Lululemon has almost single-handedly built the athleisure category while perpetuating the perception that its customers are all affluent, active, and health-focused. And who wouldn't think of Vans sneakers and associate them with skateboarding?

In the past, creating lifestyle brands was most often an opportunity to merchandise new product offerings to existing customers. Similar to *The New York Times*'s audience obsession, for brands that obsessed over offering their customers a lifestyle, they could easily expand into new product categories that aligned with that lifestyle. Today, I would argue the opportunity is even more acute. Whether a brand is going to expand into new categories or not, creating the perception of being a lifestyle brand goes hand-in-hand with being the kind of brand that provides a great experience to its customers.

CONTRIBUTING TO SOCIETAL CONVERSATIONS

Earlier in this chapter, we talked about brands being culturally relevant by breaking down the three characteristics of culture and how brands can meaningfully engage around them. The last of these—demonstrating shared beliefs—was the basis for Nike's culture-defining Colin Kaepernick campaign. However, not every brand has the opportunity to take such a meaningful stand. That does not preclude consumers from expecting brands to engage in important societal conversations, though.

In between the ephemeral, real-time marketing of Oreo and the enduring, mission-driven work of Patagonia, there are a lot of societal conversations taking place where brands are now expected to weigh in. These conversations include things that are being discussed in the media and via social media, which relate to the general mood in society. Examples are things such as **politics** (actually taking sides or simply encouraging people to vote), **legislation** (think of brands commenting on the minimum wage, transgender bathrooms, or gay marriage), **social movements** (for instance, #MeToo and Black Lives Matter), and **generational trends** (things like getting more women enrolled in STEM careers, caring for an aging population, and maternity or paternity leave from companies). In some cases, these societal conversations intersect with a brand's higher purpose—Nike with Colin Kaepernick is one such example. In many cases, however, brands are now being called on to express a point of view about societal conversations, even outside their core brand purpose.

One of the best examples of a brand contribution to societal conversations was Heineken's 2017 "Worlds Apart" demonstration—part of their larger #OpenYourWorld campaign. The activation was a leading example of what's called a social experiment where marketers pretend to be social psychologists for a day and conduct an experiment to see how people will react to certain stimuli.

In this case, the experiment brought together pairs of strangers with opposite backgrounds and opinions on divisive issues. The individuals who made up the pairs were first interviewed on camera about their opinions on divisive issues—things like feminism, climate change, and transgender identification. The pairs were deliberately cast as people who held strongly polarized views on the topic, which they expressed in their initial video interviews. The pairs were then introduced to each other and given a project to work on together. That project was, fittingly, to build a bar together.

The pairs were given simple instructions and prefabricated components to construct the bar in relatively short order. They were then prompted to have an honest conversation about themselves as people, which in all cases revealed both similarities and emotional vulnerabilities. Finally, they were shown each other's initial interview videos, where it became apparent they were fundamentally opposed to each other (a feminist was paired with a misogynist, for example). The warehouse loudspeaker offered them a choice: Leave now or sit at the bar you've just built together and discuss your differences over a beer. Thankfully, all of the pairs accepted the invitation to share a beer and discuss their differences (or at least all of the pairs who made the final cut did so).

Heineken sales skyrocketed as more than 50 million people watched this film about a social experiment between strangers. For these viewers, the emotional bond forged between strangers as they sought to understand each other over a beer was compelling as it forced them to think about their own divisive beliefs and behaviors. The real elegance in this program was that it managed to appeal to both sides of three very divisive issues. Each point of view was appropriately respected, and the ultimate societal conversation Heineken started was about understanding one another. This ad concept overall was created by Publicis, which is one of the largest advertising agencies in the world, but with strong partnership and direction from Edelman, the brand's PR firm.

Compare this with Pepsi's much maligned, purpose-pandering effort with Kendall Jenner. The same year that Heineken's social experiment captivated world audiences, Pepsi ran a mega-budget ad featuring Kendall Jenner, which aimed to connect with millennials and Gen Z who were passionate about issues surrounding racial justice and police brutality. The ad starts out by spanning an unrealistically diverse range of people, then centers on Jenner as she breaks from a picketing line to offer angry-looking police officers a can of Pepsi. The officer accepts her peace offering, and everyone is happy again. Because, you know, why hadn't we tried solving the racial justice issues in America by sharing a Pepsi before?

The ad was pulled one day after airing with criticism having already been leveled from *The New York Times*, CNN, *The Hollywood Reporter*, *Time* magazine, and dozens of other media outlets. Across social media, every possible superlative was used in admonishing the ad, and even Martin Luther King Jr.'s daughter weighed in by cynically tweeting, "If only Daddy had known the power of #Pepsi."

On the surface, these two campaigns from Heineken and Pepsi both implied a similar marketing message (drinking our product can help bring people together). The ads both imply a similar underlying insight as well—that society is currently divided, even though most people would like to find a way of coming together. The reactions to how they were executed could not have been more diametrically opposite, however. The lesson to be learned here is that the waters of societal conversation are electrically charged. If you engage in them artfully, by putting the conversation first and the brand second, as Heineken did, then society will reward you richly for contributing to an important conversation. However, if your advertising message comes across as being more important than the societal conversation, you will be punished just as severely.

EMBRACING A PURPOSEFUL MISSION

Contributing to societal conversations sheds light on an issue and should ideally exhibit a point of view from the brand. However, the conversation is inherently about society first and the brand has to find its place in the conversation secondarily. With "purpose" campaigns, those roles are reversed. This mission-oriented work starts with the brand's purpose and then seeks to explain it in the context of current society. Because this stems from the essence of the brand rather than something that's trending in society, it should be an unwavering commitment from the brand. If you're not willing to commit to something for many years, then it's probably not appropriate to engage in this kind of purpose-driven marketing.

Saying that purpose marketing requires commitment may seem a bit trite on the surface, but a lot of brands stumble here. In fact, a whole cottage industry has sprung up trying to help brands "discover their purpose" with the end result usually being advertising that misappropriates a societal issue in pursuit of marketing outcomes. For a simple example, consider Burger King's 2019 #FeelYourWay campaign, which sought to align the brand with a mental health mission. First, the campaign started from a commercial place rather than a purposeful place, by leading with "No one is Happy all the time" in a low-brow dig against McDonald's Happy Meal.

The ad then takes a strange and dark turn into a series of characters experiencing serious life events—one girl cries after being called a skank in high school, another tells her boss to go "F himself" for being a creep, while a third wonders if he will end up being alone forever. The commercial ends by saying that Burger King supports MentalHealthAmerica.net.

Source: Burger King.

Reaction to this ad wasn't quite in the Jenner-Pepsi stratosphere, but widespread condemnation followed. In this case, the condemnation centered on two things. First, it came to light that Burger King's own house wasn't in order with regard to mental health. Social media lit up with people calling on the company to offer mental health support services and insurance coverage to its employees. Second, many people rightly called the brand out for trying to align itself with a cause that had nothing to do with the brand's real purpose.

For example, on the brand's website it states, "Our commitment to premium ingredients, signature recipes, and family-friendly dining experiences is what has defined our brand for more than fifty successful years." It's easy to imagine purposeful topics that are relevant to the brand's business—encouraging positive family dynamics around the dinner table, for example, or environmental concerns related to livestock raised for its burgers. However, mental health isn't one of them. This is a great example where instead of doing something good that's born of the brand's purpose, Burger King tried forcing the brand into an unrelated cause.

Compare Burger King's haplessness with mental health to the success of skincare product philosophy, which also markets its products in connection with mental health. The difference, according to Marie Pierre Stark-Flora, who was the SVP of Brand Marketing for philosophy, is that the brand was authentically founded with a mission to improve mental well-being.

Marie-Pierre explains that the brand has its own charity called the Hope & Grace foundation, which has donated more than $5 million to supporting mental health issues and that its overall mission is, "Helping women feel good, not just look good." Speaking at Lippe Taylor's *Brand Being* event, Marie-Pierre further explained, "I don't think any other brand has literally printed statements about their purpose on every single product they've ever sold." This was no doubt an easy decision for the founder, who was herself passionate about mental wellness. However, by the time we were working with Marie-Pierre, philosophy was owned by cosmetics giant Coty, Inc. According to her, the rationale and the business case were already well established by that point, and company leadership understood the value of doing good.

"Of course, as a public company we have a lot of pressure to make the numbers. What we understood early on, though, is that emotional influence, authenticity, and generosity are a driver for business...For instance, when consumers come to the website through our Hope & Grace initiative, they spend more time on the website, they have a higher conversion rate, and they spend more money per transaction," she explained.

The brand's long-term commitment to supporting mental health initiatives is what defines their work as being a "purposeful mission" versus simply being opportunistic. Compare this with another skincare brand, Proactiv, which joined Pepsi on the list of brands mired in controversy for purpose-pandering with Kendall Jenner. In this case, the brand, which had built itself on celebrity endorsements distributed via television, was in decline and unable to connect with the new consumer. Kris Jenner approached the brand with the pitch that partnering with a different kind of celebrity—her daughter Kendall—would help them connect with young consumers again.

When it came time to announce the partnership, the brand had a meaningful story to tell—Kendall Jenner had personally experienced a significant amount of online bullying after she appeared on the red carpet with acne. However, instead of sticking to this core truth, the brand went too far in implying an even greater purpose. In teasing the announcement, Kris posted to Twitter:

 KRIS JENNER ✔️
@KRISJENNER

I'M SO PROUD OF MY DARLING @KENDALLJENNER FOR BEING SO BRAVE AND VULNERABLE. SEEING YOU SHARE HER MOST RAW STORY IN ORDER TO MAKE A POSITIVE IMPACT FOR SO MANY PEOPLE AND HELP FOSTER A POSITIVE DIALOGUE IS A TESTAMENT TO THE INCREDIBLE WOMAN YOU'VE BECOME.

Source: Jenner, Kris. Twitter Post. January 5, 2019.

The reference to braveness, vulnerability, and making a positive impact led many to hypothesize that Kendall would be revealing emotional details behind something as serious as an eating disorder or even sexual abuse. When it was instead announced she was going to appear in ads for Proactiv acne cream, the company was blasted across social media and in the press.

Lippe Taylor was engaged to help turn the situation around. We decided the best way to right the ship was to lean into Proactiv's true purpose, which is helping people feel more confident in their skin. Therefore, we partnered with Teen Vogue and concepted a program that leaned into the already existing #skinpositivity movement on Instagram. In an attempt to humanize and show Jenner's vulnerabilities, we identified negative comments posted online about her previous acne breakouts, then worked with a famous street muralist to paint the hurtful and degrading words on a building in Brooklyn.

Then we invited consumers to come join Jenner by picking up a brush and painting over the negativity until a beautiful mural emerged. Teen Vogue then hosted a live experience talking about #skinpositivity and the impact of cyberbullying on self-esteem.

The program received more than two million social media engagements and a plethora of positive press.

This program worked because we leaned into who the brand was at its core. Proactiv doesn't exist to save the earth like Patagonia or have the right to take a big stand against human trafficking like Southwest Airlines. Proactiv exists to help people get rid of their acne, and frankly, that's an important purpose, too. Starting from this core truth, it was logical and meaningful for the brand to stand on the side of #skinpositivity.

CHAPTER 5

THE FIVE FUNDAMENTAL DILEMMAS

In 2009, I had parlayed my success as a social media consultant into a job as the first head of digital marketing at a company that would later be known as W2O Group (or even later as Real Chemistry). As one of my earliest projects, every month I would fly to Minneapolis to visit General Mills, where I was helping the general counsel write policies for how brands and marketers at their company could engage in social media.

Once the policies were established, I then supported their internal center of excellence in rolling out a training program for every employee in marketing that covered everything from social media basics to best practices and rules of the road. Soon after, Yoplait stepped forward to be the first brand that funded social media-led programming for marketing purposes, thus extending the period of my regular travel to Minneapolis for the better part of two years.

It was during the annual planning process for the second year that my primary client informed me our next meeting would be in New York, instead of Minneapolis. Therefore, I left my bungalow in LA on a red-eye, cleaned up in an airport restroom, and headed straight into the glimmering offices of advertising giant Saatchi & Saatchi, New York.

The office was a beautiful, shining reminder of how many advertisements have been made by Saatchi & Saatchi over the years, and the meeting was stuffed full of two dozen people who worked on the Yoplait account. Sitting in the middle of the table was the marketing director from General Mills, and off to the side my client and I sat.

The client, market director for Yoplait, opened the meeting: "We have to bring the consumer in more. We have to listen to them. We have to embrace these new emerging channels, like social media. So for this next year's plan, I want social media to play a big part. Not only that, I want us to think differently about how we market ourselves overall."

I was enthused. For the last several years, I'd been pushing this same message and now I was hearing it straight from the decision maker's mouth. We were going to turn Yoplait into the envy of social media gurus everywhere.

The meeting was emceed by an account planner from Saatchi & Saatchi who feigned both equal enthusiasm for this innovative new direction as well as respect for the client's vision. However, over the course of the next two hours, his creative director proceeded to eviscerate everything the client wanted to do. In fact, he didn't even attempt to feign respect; he simply told the client that he was wrong.

You might think that a creative director from an esteemed ad agency like Saatchi & Saatchi would have good reasons, and it's possible that he did. But if that was the case, he couldn't be bothered to share. Instead, he impressed upon us the value of his personal expertise in selling yogurt (he had been advertising Yoplait for many years) and put forth the misguided notion that social media was where people would share and talk about his TV commercial. Nothing about it left room for discussion, debate, or data.

Now that we'd all settled that, the Don Draper parade proceeded to unveil with almost comical theatrics the new strategy for marketing Yoplait: more advertisements, but this year they would feature people "showing their joy."

I was tempted to ask why previous years had featured unhappy people, but the mood in the room was so electric that I didn't want to spoil their fun. Six months later, once these commercials were perfectly produced, this vision of showing joy wound up being a near-perfect replica of the prior year's campaign which was referred to derisively among the digital marketing team as "spooning and smiling." To learn more about this phenomenon, see the aptly titled 2016 article from The Cut headlined "A Brief History of Terrible Yogurt Commercials Targeted at Women."

Source: Gabriela Paiella, "A Brief History of Terrible Yogurt Commercials Targeted at Women," *The Cut*, June 29, 2016.

Back in the room that day, all mentions of innovation or deviating from the established advertising playbook were shut down with the one exception being that everyone agreed we could revisit the idea of including a Dad in the TV commercial down the road. Innovation indeed!

On our way back to the airport, I asked my client what had happened in the room. In particular, I was confused why a relatively senior client had been steamrolled by the creative director from his own ad agency.

My client, who was himself an employee of General Mills but someone who viewed himself as a change agent pushing for social media, was equally disappointed. He was not surprised, though. He said to me, "What you have to understand is that Saatchi has been working on this brand for a long time. The marketing director has only been on it for a brief while and will probably move onto another brand soon."

What's more, Saatchi had a direct line and powerful influence over the chief marketing officer. This marketing director may personally want to innovate, but his incentives were aligned with staying the course, making sure the brand ticked up a little bit this year, and then taking on his next assignment. And so, my client went on to explain, despite the marketing directors having theoretical authority to steward their brands, they often felt more like lame ducks when it came to disagreeing with the advertising agency.

Unfortunately, the stage was already set for Yoplait's dramatic fall. Rather than being personally responsible for the brand's problems, the bullheaded creative director was more indicative of something systematically wrong. Certainly, we can blame the agency for its hubris and dismissing the client's vision, particularly when the client had better research and a finger on the pulse of the business. However, the agency was largely incentivized by the CMO to simply improve upon last year's results. They were not being incentivized to innovate. In the same way, the marketing director was incentivized to just keep the ship steady because he would be moving on soon anyway. No one wants to create a big disruption and then leave the mess for someone else to clean up.

This anecdote may appear to be a damnation of resistance to change in ad agencies, but in truth it's an illustration that encapsulates all five of the fundamental dilemmas facing client-side brand marketers today. Many of these marketers are wrestling with significant cognitive dissonance between their personal and professional lives. As regular people, they often dislike advertising as much as the rest of us. They pay for premium content subscriptions and skip commercials whenever they can, like everyone else. They also observe the teenagers and twenty-somethings in their life dismissing advertising with an attitude that vacillates from unaware (*There was a commercial on? Sorry, I was texting*) to disdainful (*Why would they put a commercial on TikTok? It's like they've never even been here*).

What I've found from working with hundreds or thousands of brand marketers over the past fifteen years is that clients are often wedged between a rock and a hard place when it comes to making substantive changes to how their brands are marketed. As one client put it to me recently, "We say we want to innovate, but I'm not sure the company is set up for that yet."

Unfortunately, the persistent delay of innovation created the conditions for disruption, with DTC brands swooping in to wreak havoc on long-established players. For CEOs and top executives, the musical chairs happening within the marketing organization rarely means individual brand marketers are themselves left without a chair. Instead, it's the accumulation of many small refusals to change that produces systemic rot. No one individual or brand can be singled out as failures, but the environmental conditions have been set for failure on a much larger scale. For executives faced with this scenario, there are five fundamental dilemmas inside your marketing organization:

1. Measurement and Incentives
2. Commitment and Continuity
3. Proximity and Familiarity
4. Predictability and Scalability
5. Inertia and Established Beliefs

MEASUREMENT AND INCENTIVES

We're in an era where marketers are told they have to be data driven. But there's so much data that it's hard to know what to listen to. In fact, with the plethora of data available, you could literally tell any story. In this way, most marketers could look at their brand's performance and easily justify saying that "advertising is the primary growth engine responsible for our brand's success." They could also pick different data and say, "Advertising is not just a waste of resources; it's turning off consumers and decreasing our brand value." The data supports both arguments from a certain point of view. There are myriad other examples of how if the data is tortured long enough, it confesses.

On top of that, there are established measurement frameworks accepted by executive-level decision makers who are primarily responsible for resource allocation. Things like reach/frequency, GRPs, household penetration, net promoter score (NPS), cost per thousand views (CPMs), and cost per acquisition (CAC) came to dominate the last twenty years of brand marketing in large companies.

Their adoption in the C-suite has created an almost religious adherence among the rank-and-file to marketing programs that drive these metrics. The shorthand of these recognized models and the efficiency gained from having conversations in the grammar they provide were important during the era of growing through scale, when global supply chains and "boots on the ground" around the world defined corporate success.

For executives at the top, the value of these frameworks is obvious. Having a standardized view makes it easier to determine who should get more resources. Unfortunately, for the people executing marketing programs, the impact is more reminiscent of the infamous "cobra effect" when the British government was concerned with the number of venomous cobras in India. The well-intentioned incentive of a bounty paid for every dead cobra instead led to the widespread and seriously dangerous reaction of Indians raising cobras just to turn them in. Marketers who are incentivized to deliver GRPs will buy more TV commercials. Those who are incentivized to maximize CPMs will buy cheap influencer posts. And when asked to optimize NPS, they will focus on current customers instead of acquiring new ones.

These measurement frameworks serve an important purpose for top executives to evaluate performance across categories, brands, and geographies. However, they are also preventing brand marketers from using their own judgment, trying something new, and competing with the speed and agility of smaller competitors.

Of course, many companies have adopted more sophisticated multi-touch attribution modeling, which attempts to define how various marketing levers contribute to a chosen success variable, such as sales. These multivariate regressions do a better job of showing the individual contribution of many different levers being pulled in complex marketing programs. However, to be effective these models need a lot of data (at least a year, often two years) and they fail to account for the nuance in things such as consumer sentiment, reputation, and perception.

Many brand marketers have bemoaned the issue of measurement and incentives, but there isn't any "new age" framework to adopt. Any framework would eventually wind up with the same issues, and the time required to drive adoption throughout a large company would itself be a massive drain on resources and focus. Most often, when presented with these obstacles, company executives decide what they have is good enough and continue making small, incremental changes while searching through their ranks for that person or people who can deliver lightning in a bottle despite the deck being stacked against them.

Time and again, I hear these executives—CEOs, Presidents, CMOs—say, "My twenty-five-year-old daughter does this, but that's not how we're marketing our brands." Unfortunately, they don't have a measurement framework for her snapchatting or their son connected-gaming with all his friends. Meanwhile, smaller companies where the executives interact directly with the marketers on a daily basis are able to allocate resources based on observation and lived experiences, rather than waiting for something to show up in next year's measurement report.

Perhaps the best illustration of this difference comes from Monster Energy and Red Bull. I have worked with both companies over the course of my career, interacting directly with the C-suite for both. The difference in how they measure success is worth talking about. With Monster Energy, every month we reviewed measurement scorecards that compared social media conversation about Monster with Red Bull. Those scorecards rolled up into a larger measurement report that included broader marketing measures as well as sales and was presented to top leadership.

At Red Bull, I spent a year and a half working on-site from their offices every week, rolling out a company-wide measurement platform. Not once did we talk about Monster Energy. It wasn't even in the scorecards. And not once did we roll up our measurement scores to a single, executive-level view. Our measurement approach was to empower the teams on the ground with daily information about how they were performing in specific communities. The Culture Team looked at measures of how Red Bull was being discussed within the breakdancing and beatboxing community. The Extreme Sports Team did the same within skateboarding and snowboarding. And so on throughout the hundreds of marketers around the company.

Red Bull's philosophy was to become part of culture. They were creating a lifestyle brand, and they empowered their marketers to make resource allocation decisions. There was never a conversation about measuring individual pieces of content or trying to drive CPMs from every single post. The mentality was simple: be among the consumers, give the consumers what they want, entertain them, create opportunities for them to be inspired. And Monster Energy? Who cared about your competitor when your job was to live the Red Bull lifestyle? That was the best example I've ever seen of marketing to consumers on their own terms. It's an approach that has been reinforced repeatedly by Jeff Bezos. In a speech delivered to the Economic Club of Washington in September 2018, he explained, "The number one thing that has made us successful by far is obsessive compulsive focus on the customer as opposed to obsession over the competitor."

Back in Minneapolis, as we continued the planning process for Yoplait's big "showing joy" campaign, it became clear why the people in that room were so dismissive of social media. Every mention of how the program would be measured came back to GRPs. If you wanted to succeed at Yoplait, you had to drive GRPs.

Eighteen months later, an article in *Entrepreneur* magazine headlined "How Chobani Yogurt Used Social Media to Boost Sales" announced that Chobani was approaching $1 billion in annual sales thanks to a "highly effective marketing and social media strategy that has catapulted it to the top of its industry."[49] The only measurement method cited in the article besides sales growth was termed "brand engagement."

49 Samuel Greengard, "How Chobani Yogurt Used Social Media to Boost Sales,' *Entrepreneur,* last modified September 16, 2012, https://www.entrepreneur.com/article/223999.

COMMITMENT AND CONTINUITY

Commitment is a tough word for marketers today. It brings to mind marriage, but unlike marriage, the notion of sticking with something "for better or for worse" in marketing sounds like being foolishly bullheaded. Why stick with something that's obviously not working? However, any decent transformation consultant will tell you change takes time, and it takes even more time to reap the rewards from that change. The dilemma facing marketers is, they have an unprecedented number of options to choose from, and they have been brought up in the school of "test and learn." There is of course plenty of sense in testing and learning, but in recent years the concept has been taken to an extreme. Couple this with the atomization of vendors and marketing philosophies, and marketers could literally be testing (and learning!) something new every day.

For marketers who have traditionally relied heavily on advertising, the trends described in this book require a wholesale transformation. It won't work to simply repurpose advertising dollars into another proven tactic. The new marketing that consumers want is much more fragmented, nuanced, and requires a new emphasis on people resources rather than just buying media. This kind of transformation will inevitably lead to variable results in the short term. However, the longer brands continue investing in a depreciating asset, which advertising has become, the less the reward will be once they finally transform themselves.

All this is to say that transformative change requires commitment. Thankfully, we are beyond the point where this kind of transformative change required a large leap of faith. Now the question is more about how and when to leap instead of whether to do so.

No matter how this happens for your company, committing

to a strategic North Star is the most important determinant of success with major change. Perhaps the best example is Amazon's commitment to Prime. As explained to me by David "Ech" Echegoyen, who was the Chief Customer Officer at Jet.com while the ecommerce startup skyrocketed to a billion dollars of revenue in just two years, "the genius of Amazon Prime is that it became the decision-making filter for everything at Amazon... If we do this, will it attract more people to register for Prime?" Ech went on to say, "This is how Amazon knew to get into free music streaming, original TV productions, and any number of other things. By offering them to consumers, they could get more Prime subscribers."

This kind of North Star usually needs both senior support as well as a champion to drive ongoing commitment. It means somebody stepping up in every meeting and saying, "This sounds like an interesting idea...but how does it align with our North Star?" Unfortunately, in many large companies, marketing roles don't have the continuity that's necessary for this kind of commitment. In fact, rotating brand marketers is seen as a best practice. Doing so is meant to bring in fresh thinking, expose rising stars to different challenges, and also prevent any one person from screwing up a brand with a hundred years of heritage. The result, however, is that no one ever commits to a brand long enough to drive transformative change.

One of the first things my client at General Mills mentioned as we were driving away from Saatchi headquarters was the relatively brief amount of time the Yoplait marketing director would be spending on the brand. It could be argued, as my colleague did, that with such a short stint planned, the Yoplait marketing director simply didn't want to pick this battle. If he was planning to stay on the brand for another five years, maybe he would have realized the importance of innovating and investing in new areas such as social media. However, given his tenure was likely to be less than two years, he was mostly incentivized to tweak the existing formula, do slightly better than his predecessor, and then move on.

I saw this later at Hershey. It was 2012 and the meeting that brought me there was with the marketing director for the Hershey brand at that time. The pitch went great and the internal digital marketing leader was practically certain we had convinced him to make a meaningful investment in social media marketing. After seeing our analysis and case study of how we had helped Reese's reach six million fans—SIX MILLION!—without spending a dollar on paid media, it seemed like a total no-brainer.

The marketing director and I remained behind after everyone else had left the room, and he said to me flat out, "Paul, that was a great presentation. But I have to tell you...we're not going to do it." I was more than a little disappointed; in fact, it's one of those moments that has stayed with me, clear as day for almost a decade. "It's great what you're doing with Reese's," he continued. "But this is Hershey. It's been around a hundred years, and here I am. My job isn't to innovate. My job is to not be the guy who screwed it up."

This may sound like the story of a corporate suit who just wanted to cover his own ass, or like a classic example of systemic resistance to change. But when this same marketing director moved off the brand, his very next job was to launch Brookside Chocolate. This was an innovation brand, and by all accounts, he made a massive success of it.

Certainly, there is an entrenched reverence for top brands like Hershey—brands that literally have a town named after them.

However, this marketing director also knew his time on the brand would be relatively brief. How could he be the one who caused disruption if he wasn't going to be there to see it through? There's no doubt this lack of continuity and tenure from brand marketers has kept many established brands in a holding pattern.

What would it look like to build continuity into a brand marketing role? That's for each company to decide. But here's something to think about. Meaningful change in resource allocation is needed for brands to adapt to the post-advertising world. Shifting resources away from traditional ads in favor of putting the consumer first and marketing with purpose-driven, culturally relevant, and social media-led campaigns is quite literally the only option for most large brands to compete today and in the future. However, that doesn't mean the first six months or even the first year of this change are going to demonstrate immediate results. Like most transformation efforts, you have to make a long-term commitment if you want to future-proof your marketing, and that means putting people in place who will be committed to seeing the change through.

PROXIMITY AND FAMILIARITY

I interview hundreds of job candidates each year and have for many years now. Almost every time, I ask them to name a brand that does a good job of marketing to "somebody like them." Invariably, if the candidate is a young millennial or Gen Z woman, she will probably say Glossier. It's become something of an experiment at this point—it doesn't matter if the candidate is interviewing for a job in the Beauty, Consumer, Healthcare, or Financial Services sector. She's equally likely to name Glossier as the brand that "gets" her. But that's because Glossier really is run by people like her. And it feels like it. Their tone is exactly right. They are on trend as things happen. They engage directly in personal interactions with their customers.

One of the challenges with large brands in particular is that the decision makers often have nothing in common with the audience they're trying to market to. Of course this is intimately connected to the lack of diversity and representation in senior roles across corporate America. However, it's not limited to situations where white males are trying to market to diverse audiences. When I worked with Viagra, their target was sixty-five-plus years old, predominantly white men, and the entire brand team consisted of Asian American women in their thirties.

Is it possible for brand marketers to get the tone, messaging, timing, and overall brand relevance right without *being* the consumer they're trying to reach? Absolutely. But the bar has been raised in consumer's minds. The wave of brands like Glossier—brands that were started by a founder who is marketing to people just like themselves—has created much higher expectations in consumers' minds. In describing the success of Jet.com, which Walmart acquired for $3 billion, Chief Customer Officer David Echegoyen told me, "In different places you're trying to sell something to a customer that's hard to relate to. For us, most of our employees find it easy to relate to the challenges of our customer." Ech himself was born in El Salvador and came to the United States as an eighteen-year-old. Since then, he's lived in parts of America as diverse as New York and Arkansas. As the decision maker for Jet.com's marketing efforts, he told me the key to his success was to empower people to pursue their ideas even if he didn't think they were going to work.

This idea of empowerment is easy for senior leaders to embrace intellectually but very difficult to support in practice. In particular, for decision makers who are marketing to an audience that's different from themselves, the key is to hire, empower, and listen to people who represent that audience. Very often, that means putting great trust in the seemingly untested opinions of young people. In every instance, it means also listening to your consumers much more intimately than most big company executives are accustomed to doing.

Returning to Yoplait, consider the fact that Yoplait was churning out over a billion cups of yogurt a year at that time, making it the entrenched market leader. However, the President of the business unit was far removed from his actual customers. In fact, when we presented data from social listening and personal experience about young consumer's affection for Greek yogurt, he dismissed the trend as something for coastal elites, scoffing that Middle America would never go for something so *European*.

As someone who had succeeded in his career by knowing the consumer, it didn't occur to him that he had grown disconnected and was no longer familiar with today's consumer. By the time he was fired, Greek yogurt represented 20 percent of the total yogurt market and Yoplait had ceded its number one position. General Mills later went on to implement a social listening program across its brands.

This failure from a lack of proximity and familiarity with the consumer is not limited to corporate environments. It's also common in traditional advertising environments. Despite the impression that agencies are the domain of youth, most creative teams in advertising agencies follow strict protocols about who can pitch ideas and who has final approval rights. The more seasoned creative directors are almost always the decision makers. They are also overwhelmingly white men (the advertising industry has grappled with its lack of diversity for years, leading to the launch of the 3 percent movement in response to the shocking revelation that only 3 percent of creative directors were women), and most of them grew up in the television era, where they were trained to operate in a traditional paid media ecosystem.

In 2019, Lippe Taylor was working closely with the Mucinex brand to try and create greater relevance with young consumers. The brand was a sales powerhouse in drugstore channels and famous for its ads including Mr. Mucus. However, that combination of retail shelf presence and traditional advertising were not translating to relevance among Gen Z.

The brand received a jolt of inspiration when Cynthia Chen joined as the general manager, and our pitch to be the first OTC healthcare brand on TikTok was suddenly embraced. However, as with most large, heritage brands, we operated in an IAT (integrated agency team) environment and McCann Health, the largest advertising agency in the world, was considered their lead agency. Therefore, McCann got the nod to deliver a great creative idea for reaching Gen Z on TikTok.

The ensuing campaign was called #TooSickToBeSick and it was the first OTC health campaign ever on TikTok. Significant paid media investment bought enough impressions to call it a moderate success, and it was heralded as a breakthrough innovation throughout the halls of McCann. But the creative concept was a dud. The campaign featured TikTok influencers pretending to be sick with a cold, then transforming into their "sick" well-dressed selves going out for the night. (Get it? *Sick* can also mean *cool*—see what they did there?)

The campaign wreaked of a disconnected Dad trying to emulate his daughter on social media. It was clear the approval process at McCann had ended with a senior creative leader who didn't have enough proximity or familiarity with the audience and who exerted too much influence over the team members who did.

Thankfully, the brand still had enthusiasm for innovating further to reach young consumers, and for the second go-round, they gave the opportunity to Lippe Taylor. After seeing McCann's struggles to connect, we decided not to follow a traditional creative process. Our creative team still led the overall ideation, but they chose to collaborate in close partnership with an influencer pair who were themselves wildly successful on TikTok (husband-wife team Allison and Twitch). Therefore, not only did we ensure the work was led by members of our creative team who had proximity and familiarity with the Gen Z audience, but we were also getting direct input and partnership from creators who defined that kind of familiarity with audiences on the platform.

The ensuing campaign, #BeatTheZombieFunk, leaned into the brand's strategy of showing that Mucinex can cure your symptoms at night, while allowing you to wake up feeling human in the morning (not like a zombie). The production, influencer casting, and all the supporting materials were either written or heavily informed by Gen Z and young millennials on our creative and influencer teams, who were themselves TikTok users. The internal approval process was more about guiding them to their best thinking rather than telling them what to say.

The result is that #BeatTheZombieFunk became the number one, most engaged brand campaign ever on TikTok. More than a million young consumers actively participated—recording and posting videos that tagged Mucinex. As the CEO of Lippe Taylor, I looked at the campaign and saw a dozen little tweaks that I might have made to it. Thankfully, I didn't. Otherwise, it might have come out sounding like a disconnected Dad trying to emulate one of his daughters on social media.

SCALABILITY AND PREDICTABILITY

Despite my setback at Hershey, I was having a lot of success in 2012 convincing companies to commit more resources to social media marketing. One of my greatest successes was on the other side of the country, where *Fast Company* had recently named Intel one of the most innovative companies in social media. Becky Brown was the internal leader tasked with steering Intel's social media efforts, and she considered us her agency of record. I was the most senior and hands-on consultant working with them at that time, and so I'd been called to an annual planning meeting held in Portland with all their global marketers in attendance either physically or virtually. One of the other presenters at this meeting came from Facebook—a platform where we had helped Intel amass over 20 million fans on the backs of a great content and community-first strategy. Facebook was nearing its IPO, and we were nervous the pressures of the street would lead to a decreased emphasis on community while the company made its pitch to advertisers. In hindsight, all those fears and then some came true.

Back at the meeting in Portland, Facebook's representative unveiled the company's new pitch: advertising on Facebook offered marketers the same persuasiveness as earned media with the scale and predictability of paid media. It was a bold claim that assumed and conflated several things. Most importantly, it assumed the two media formats were as she claimed: paid media was scalable and predictable while earned media was persuasive.

In many ways, the pitch accurately described the historical truths about earned and paid media. Earned media has always been more persuasive, which our *Friction Fatigue Report* reinforced by finding that more than 70 percent of all consumers believe editorial articles about a product are more trustworthy than advertisements. However, the scalability and predictability of paid media is what powered Big Advertising's growth while public relations remained relatively small by comparison.

The scalability claim is true on the one hand but is also misguided. It's true that brands can buy literally endless advertising inventory, while editorial space for their products is extremely limited. However, with the vast majority of advertising underperforming, one has to question the wisdom of buying so much scale. P&G again provided a window into this dilemma when, in 2017, CEO David Taylor announced the company had cut $100 million in advertising over just one quarter and saw no impact on their brands' growth rates.

On the flip side, engaging marketing programs are finding greater scale than ever before in the form of consumers sharing and talking about them. This is evidenced by all the great marketing success stories mentioned throughout this book.

When considering the predictability of advertising, the picture is considerably more nuanced. By 2012, all of this was starting to change, and by 2021, that change has manifested itself. As the modern, ad-averse consumer has replaced last century's couch potato, the predictability of advertising-led growth has plummeted. Most notably, as we saw in Chapter 1, Kantar reported in 2019 that less than 25 percent of the year's award-winning television ads provided brand impact over the short or long term. The belief that advertising is a predictable growth driver is outdated. Why, then, do so many marketers rely on it to such an extent?[50]

Almost all marketers at large companies endeavor under annual budgeting cycles. Their corporate finance team allocates budget based on need and performance. Sometimes a brand receives more budget because it's underperforming and needs to catch up, sometimes because it's overperforming and more budget would deliver further growth. Either way, receiving more budget is based on predicting future sales. And the internally established frameworks for predicting sales often rely on forecasted advertising spend. Therefore, in order to get more budget, brands are literally forced into predicting a future with more advertising. Although it's true that many companies have internal innovation budgets and *Shark Tank*-like competitions, the ability to receive funding outside of the core, advertising-supported sales forecasts is severely limited.

Thus, the emphasis on advertising is built into the system for many marketers. Consider a recent brand plan for a leading product in health and wellness. The promotions budget for this brand was $20 million with $15 million being slated for advertising. Naturally, in circumstances like this, the brand team and senior executives therefore believe the advertising is their most important marketing effort, and it becomes the defining initiative for their overall marketing strategy. Other efforts, such as public relations, social media, and influencer marketing, are only discussed AFTER the advertising concept has already been decided.

There's no problem with using scalable marketing channels to

50 Barry Levine, "Kantar: Award-Winning Ads Are Becoming Less Effective at Brand Building," Marketing Dive, September 26, 2019, https://www.marketingdive.com/news/kantar-award-winning-ads-are-becoming-less-effective-at-brand-building/563758/.

achieve your goals, especially for large brands. The problem is when brands let the size of their investment dictate the relative importance of their marketing initiatives. In fact, that's exactly how we arrived at this place where TV commercials became equated with "above the line" (ATL) advertising while everything else was deemed "below the line" (BTL). This framework, like many of the most widely accepted practices in marketing today, was popularized by Procter & Gamble in the twentieth century. It initially existed to delineate the agencies they would pay higher fees to—ATL agencies—versus those that were simply repurposing creative ideas into smaller, less impactful marketing channels.

Unfortunately, like many P&G frameworks that built high-value brands last century, this notion of designing a whole marketing program around an ATL advertising campaign is not only outdated, but it is also responsible for holding many brand marketers back. The planning cycle and framework around ATL concepts has in fact turned many brands into advertising ouroboros (the mythical snake or dragon that bites its own tail) in which their forecasts are dependent on ATL advertising spend; therefore, they prioritize their ATL advertising plan. These companies are getting disrupted by challenger brands that never bit their own tail; therefore, they're able to glide between more nimble marketing programs.

The Facebook rep's assertion that scalability and predictability are the root of marketer's desires was accurate. The problem is that advertising's success is not nearly as predictable as it used to be—as evidenced by Kantar's findings. Meanwhile, marketing programs that engender earned media and social sharing are more scalable than ever before. Old Spice demonstrated the sheer volume that can be generated with the right kind of program.

Their scale came from earned media coverage and social media sharing of the response videos, rather than via the advertising.

We're going to talk in Chapter 6 about how brands can approach their planning cycle differently. But perhaps the most important thing is to overcome this dilemma of scalability and predictability. Rather than accepting the old wisdom that advertising is scalable and predictable, acknowledge the rapidly changing reality that it's far less predictable than it used to be, and it's not the right kind of scale for engaging the modern consumer.

INERTIA AND ESTABLISHED BELIEFS

At the December 2009 Open Innovation Summit, a panel discussion among innovation leaders at HP, Clorox, and Shell discussed the "immune system" possessed by large companies. They talked about how this make-believe system often activates people termed "corporate antibodies," who purposefully stifle new or outside ideas. This idea of corporate antibodies has found a foothold in management consulting and transformation teams who feel targeted by invisible and often passive-aggressive resistance to new ideas or beliefs. At Yoplait, it was the ad agency's creative director who imposed inertia and established beliefs on the brand. But the impact was the same.

It's no great insight that large companies suffer from inertia and struggle with changing long-established beliefs. However, for brand marketers who suffer from cognitive dissonance between their own lived experience with marketing (skipping, blocking, and eliminating advertisements in their personal lives) and the investments they make professionally (still putting large investments into advertising), there are specific beliefs that are protected by corporate antibodies which make change in their companies very difficult. They are:

1. Working versus Nonworking Dollars
2. Matching Luggage with Reach and Frequency
3. Best Practices

To tackle these established beliefs in order, let's start with what is perhaps the most undermining belief for brands wanting to reach the modern consumer. This is what's known as "working" versus "nonworking" dollars.

For many marketers who grew up in the advertising-led marketing world, this concept of working versus nonworking dollars became a popular way of saying, the ad agency needs to limit how much money it pays itself for making an ad and maximize how much money is spent placing that ad where people can see it. One has to assume that salespeople from publishers and media buying agencies played a role in promoting what came to be taken as fact—that resources spent on things such as creativity and making marketing materials should be limited to a small percentage of the total resources being spent on advertising space with media outlets.

Many large companies, especially CPG companies, have established specific target ratios for working versus nonworking dollars, which are reviewed and even enforced by procurement departments. The problem is, not only were the ratios established under a different era of old-school advertising, but also the very definition of what constitutes "working" investment in new media channels is different.

Bryan Wiener, then-CEO of 360i, noted in a 2016 article for

AdAge that "the upside to replacing the working versus non-working ratio metric will lead to an increase in great work outside of the traditional box of paid media,"[51] and the inverse is also true: "The downside of not replacing the working versus non-working metric will lead to an increase in work that does not work well."

Wiener is correct. The relentless efforts of large marketers to rein in spending on creative talent has played a role in why advertising is no longer as effective as it once was. However, even more importantly, consumers want marketing that involves a more personal touch today. The PwC report on customer experience found that 82 percent of people want more human interaction with brands. This aligns with what we've seen from Samsung mobile's community management program and DTC brands like Glossier engaging directly with consumers. Consumers appreciate brands that spend resources on real people engaging with them, as opposed to buying more paid media. However, this kind of human engagement requires a different kind of resourcing.

Research from Exane BNP Paribas found that while traditional advertising should have a ratio of 55–60 percent "working" dollars (paid media) to 40–45 percent "nonworking" dollars (creative, production), when considering social media that ratio should instead be 12 percent "working" (paid media) to 88 percent "nonworking" (listening, creative, content, community management).

---

51   Tom Finneran, "Dispelling the Myth of Working vs. Non-working Marketing Spending," *AdAge,* January 7, 2016, https://adage.com/article/guest-columnists/dispelling-myth-working-working-ratio/302023.

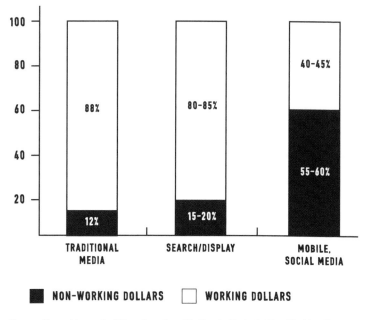

Source: Peggy Munnagle, "More than Ever, It's Time to Evaluate Non-Working Marketing Spend," Quad, February 18, 2021.

This distinction illustrates the challenge with allowing established beliefs such as what constitutes "working" dollars to define your marketing efforts. If money spent on engaging consumers in social media is not considered "working" by your organization, then why would anyone spend 88 percent of their resources on it? People resources, whether with an agency or in-house, that are spent engaging consumers are in fact "working" in social media. Perhaps most importantly, the very concept of "working" versus "nonworking" dollars has become antiquated, and the definitions themselves are working to hold many brands back.

Our next example of how established beliefs can lead to systemic and counterproductive inertia is the ad agency-promoted concept of "matching luggage" paired with their media buying partner's favorite claims about reach/frequency. Taken together, the notion is that all brand marketing assets ought to look the same (which supports the ad agency's desire to be the agency producing as many marketing assets as possible) and that simply exposing consumers to your message enough times (usually six or more) will lead to them taking action (never mind that beating people over the head with your ads just compounds their irritation).

The truth is that matching luggage marketing looks oddly out of place in social media feeds. In fact, when you consider the social media-leading brand Away (which sells actual luggage), you'll find a wide array of visual depictions in their feeds. The images range from filtered to unfiltered, gritty to polished, illustrated to photographed, branded to unbranded, and meme-like to magazine-like. The way they reach people is by being relevant in their feeds at that moment, not by forcing a consistent brand style on their followers. In a world where the majority of people have developed "blindness" to branded advertisements, this ability to make marketing content frictionless by blending into consumer's feeds is far more important than the theory of "matching luggage" for visual branding.

Finally, let's talk about best practices. While writing this chapter of the book, a marketing client bemoaned to me the impossible hypocrisy of her leadership's expectations. Leadership, she explained, had tasked her team with delivering industry "firsts" in marketing—for example, being the first to try out a new activation on TikTok. Then every time she proposed a new idea, leadership would ask to see examples of how it worked and wanted clear expectations of what metrics they could expect from it.

Unfortunately, you can't have both innovation and certainty.

Marketing as an industry has exploded over the last twenty years, and brands now have more diverse and frenetic competition than ever before. Anytime you are clinging to a model of how things ought to be done, you are creating the conditions for disruption. Thus, while marketers are conditioned to seek out these "best practices," clear KPIs, and case studies of prior success before investing in new initiatives, once these proof points exist, the initiative is already going to be less effective than the case studies being used as examples.

This is both an exciting and also intimidating prospect for most brand marketers today because exploring new territory and embracing untested ideas is the surest way to get outsized results.

THE DYNAMICS OF THE DILEMMAS

These dilemmas aren't going away anytime soon. So in all likelihood, most marketers could continue to earn their annual bonuses if they keep doing things the old way, in perpetuity. But at some point, their brand will be completely disrupted by a company whose marketers are not doing it the old way. For this reason, it is the five fundamental dilemmas, much more than specific disruptions such as ecommerce or DTC brands, that ultimately lead to brands getting disrupted. If not for the dilemmas, entrenched market leaders would have a much better shot of evolving their own approaches rather than allowing someone else to come in from the outside.

Do you really think Gillette couldn't have figured out a better way of selling razors? And yet they kept doing it the same way, year after year putting out celebrity-laden advertisements, all while the consumer experience became worse and worse. Each new product launch made it harder and harder to understand which specific razor to purchase. Consumers would walk into the drugstore and be overwhelmed by the many options that were obviously born out of focusing on the competition rather than the customer (as a customer, why should I want titanium versus rhodium blades?). Product marketing claims became increasingly untethered from factual evidence (how do I know this razor lifts the hairs before it cuts them? Is it really going to be the closest shave I've ever had?). And then on top of it, because they had confused the retailer for the customer, the darn things were locked up with theft prevention devices that might as well be renamed "positive experience prevention" devices. Gillette was so insulated in their world that it's no surprise Dollar Shave Club came along and completely disrupted them.

There are thousands of brands out there following in Gillette's (and Yoplait's) footsteps. They have short-term incentives measured by overly reductive KPIs. The people on the brand are frequently cycling on and off. They're told to innovate but that they should also follow best practices, and that ideas are only valuable if they scale. In many cases, they're not close to or familiar with the consumer they're marketing to. On top of it, they're adhering to established beliefs that were born in a very different era.

These dilemmas may not be fully surmountable, but even within these constraints, brand marketers can think and operate differently. Doing so will make a world of difference in enabling them to deliver the kind of marketing experiences that consumers want to engage with. That is the crucial topic of the next chapter in which we will explore a specific framework for frictionless marketing.

CHAPTER 6

MAKING MARKETING FRICTIONLESS

Throughout this book, we have seen how advertising rose to prominence and lost its ability to connect with consumers. We have seen how Google and Facebook forced the media industry to become overly reliant on Big Advertising, leading to a terrible experience for consumers. And how those media companies have turned to a new, audience-obsessed philosophy that will benefit consumers over marketers. We've also seen the kind of marketing those consumers want to engage with—marketing that fits in their lives without interrupting or intruding upon them. Marketing that is frictionless rather than disruptive. Finally, we've looked at the dilemmas inside of large companies that make it difficult and have delayed marketers from offering consumers the kind of marketing experience they want. Now in this chapter, I will offer a new framework for how marketers might overcome these obstacles and leverage the trends among consumers and media to their benefit.

OFFERING A NEW FRAMEWORK

Outside of the office, I am a lifetime soccer player and fan. Before either of my daughters could walk, they could both kick a soccer ball. Laces first—not with their toe. In fact, this is one of the first things young children are taught when learning to play soccer. The natural inclination as a child is to kick the ball as hard and far as they can. After experimenting a little, they usually discover they can kick the farthest by smashing the point of their toe into the ball. Of course, they have very little control over how the ball flies or where it lands, but "toeing it" certainly delivers a fast boost. This is where coaches come in to help young players overcome the urge to smash it with their toe and learn to strike the ball with finesse and accuracy.

Soccer is known around the world as the "beautiful game" because despite being a contact sport, it is remarkably *friction-less*. You can watch a full ninety minutes and the ball almost never stops as it pings around the pitch. In fact, this is one reason why soccer has been slow to advance in the United States. American sports are subsidized by advertising, and advertisers LOVE interrupting sporting events to broadcast commercial messages. Baseball, basketball, and football all offer frequent timeouts and other breaks in the action—friction points, if you will, where advertisers can insert their interruptions. Even hockey is a relatively short game with two extended commercial breaks between periods. Soccer has only one break, halftime, which appeals much less to advertisers than frequent, in-game interruptions.

Leading your marketing campaign with Big Advertising is like kicking a soccer ball with your big toe. It injects a lot of momentum into the campaign but with very little nuance and very little control over how it's going to fly or where it's going to land. By comparison, the world's best soccer players demonstrate extraordinary control and frictionless passing as the ball zips around between teammates. Although they occasionally kick the ball with their toe, it's always a last resort.

Therefore, it seems a fitting analogy to base the framework for how we rethink marketing away from using the big toe of advertising and instead learning to kick it with our LACES.

KICKING IT WITH THE LACES:

- **L**isten extensively
- **A**ctivate, don't advertise
- **C**ollaborate as a strategy
- **E**ngage your audiences; don't target them
- **S**cale your program as the last thing you do

LISTENING IS MORE IMPORTANT THAN TALKING

Epictetus, a Greek philosopher who spent his youth as a slave in Rome before gaining freedom after the death of Nero, is famous for having said, "We have two ears and one mouth so that we might listen twice as much as we speak."

As a brand marketer, think about how much time you spend working on message development, perfecting calls to action, and optimizing the places those messages appear. Now compare that with how much time you spend listening to your consumer. More than 75 percent of consumers surveyed for the *Friction Fatigue Report* agreed, *when I post something about a brand online, I expect them to be listening.* That number increases among frequent posters and Gen Xers. Meanwhile, many of the best marketing success stories in recent history were born out of listening to consumers, and yet very few marketers devote meaningful time to listening.

Kelley Sternhagen is now a vice-president of marketing strategy at Cost Plus World Market, but she started her marketing career on my social listening team at W2O Group. For one of her assignments, she spent a whole year deployed on-site at Nike's headquarters in Portland, helping them listen to their consumers ahead of the 2014 World Cup. This kind of commitment—to having a full-time person listening on a daily basis—is what it takes to really understand your consumer. Kelley explained her experience to me by saying, "At Nike, the amount of senior-level attention that was placed on social listening was intense. Almost every week, I was being asked to present the latest on what consumers were talking about."

Because I realize "listen to your consumer" is a bit of a trite and finger-wagging recommendation, let me go a step further by suggesting how marketers might embrace more of the Nike approach in their listening efforts today.

First, commit to listening as a strategic imperative. This means putting resources and time against it. It could be a fully dedicated Listening Lab or just an internal person who has listening in their job title. It's something you should be committed to within your internal team, though, in addition to relying on one or more agency partners to help you.

Second, ensure you're listening to anyone you can. We've focused a lot on consumers in this book, but you will discover valuable insights by listening everywhere. Listen to your distributors or retailers, sales leaders, customer service reps, and your internal team members, all the way down to the interns.

Third, make listening an active part of your schedule every week. This means changing from an annual, quarterly, or monthly market research report to a weekly pulse check. This is a philosophical shift away from landing on one big insight and developing a whole marketing plan around it. Think of it instead like a constant commitment to learning and improving with new inputs. Because of this, you can also limit the number of data points you look at every week. Don't look at every measure at once because you'll never absorb the full power of an insight if you're trying to digest a dozen different data points. Now that you're doing weekly pulse checks, you can rotate your attention between different data points each week and think about what they mean.

Fourth, resist the urge to overstructure and overoperationalize your listening project. No doubt you have market researchers who are brilliant at creating statistically valid studies, but any effort where you control all the variables is not really listening.

Finally, keep a Listening Log of interesting things you've heard.

They don't need to be breakthrough insights. It's more about maintaining a list of things that stood out to you because someday, they will likely tell a story. Without the Listening Log, you will likely forget things that could be much more valuable when put into different context down the road.

The three biggest reasons I see brand marketers underresource their listening efforts are lack of predictability, lack of time, and desire to put their resources into "working" dollars.

I can't guarantee what kind of value you will derive from listening, but I can guarantee you will get out what you put into it. Although less predictable than most marketers would like, the value from listening can impact your product innovations, marketing campaigns, pricing strategy, competitive positioning, cultural relevance, ability to avoid negative issues, and so much more. You won't know what value awaits before you dive in, but the juice is worth the squeeze.

When it comes to not having enough time in the day, this is more about how you structure your listening program. I recommend having an internal resource dedicated to it, with support from an agency as well. As the brand marketer, you can consume the information in whatever format works best for you—whether that's weekly meetings, text updates as they happen, or a voice recording about the latest findings you can listen to en route to the airport. However you set it up, committing to listening yourself is more than half the battle.

It's also important to note the "working dollars" fallacy discussed in Chapter 5 can often lead to the dangerous belief that agencies should provide research and insights for free to their clients. I say this is dangerous because it leads agencies to prioritize data and insights that support their own ideas. If the client isn't paying for it anyway, it indicates the client doesn't value the data. They only value the creative ideas, and they want the comfort of knowing their agency used data to arrive at the ideas. This kind of thinking will hold your own internal team back. It will increase the likelihood that the data you see has been cherry-picked, and it will greatly diminish your ability to apply the insights to other parts of your business. You get what you pay for—and it's worth it to pay for good listening.

Finally, remember that listening should be a client-side priority, supported by technology and your agency partners. But it's your data and your insights. If this means moving dollars from your paid media plan to cover listening, then it's worth it. There's no doubt you have spend that's not working as hard as you want, and now could be the time to divert those resources into an effort that will improve the entire spectrum of your marketing mix.

ACTIVATE, DON'T ADVERTISE

Between 2008 and 2020, Dr. Pepper awarded more than $10 million in college tuition grants or scholarships to college students. These scholarships are part of a massive sponsorship with NCAA sports. For those who watch college football games, it's impossible not to be drawn in as Saturday afternoon halftime shows depict college students breaking into tears of joy as Dr. Pepper reveals they never have to worry about student loans again. The scholarships are awarded right on the field and serve to draw viewers' attention back to their television sets after they wandered into the kitchen during the commercial break.

Dr. Pepper is a huge hero in this program, which demonstrates the brand's commitment to supporting college students on an issue that's important to them. Additionally, there are entertaining components such as the Halftime Challenge where the students (who are typically NOT college athletes) compete for tuition money by throwing footballs into giant Dr. Pepper cans, and there is a user-generated content aspect where students upload videos of themselves describing how they will make an impact with their degree and how the scholarship from Dr. Pepper will impact their community and the world. Mentioning Dr. Pepper in the videos is encouraged but not required.

In addition to this incredible marketing activation, Dr. Pepper also introduced the Fansville advertising campaign. This campaign, which has been widely lauded in advertising award shows, includes nine different commercials culminating in a "season finale" designed to create the impression of an actual television series where every character wears Dr. Pepper-branded apparel and loves football. As television commercials go, it's an entertaining and engaging campaign. However, it's also nine different television commercials shot by an Emmy-winning director and including multiple celebrities (Brian Bosworth and Eddie George, for example, who are college football heroes). In other words, a breathtaking amount of money went into producing this ad campaign.

According to the agency's award entry for Cannes Lion consideration, the commercials were aired so many times that they reached over one billion impressions in a single year. To drive home the point, Dr. Pepper spent well more than ten times as much money on the advertising campaign as they did on the scholarship activation. Analyzing this campaign against the brand's objectives, it appears the effort was a success. Dr. Pepper sales increased 3.7 percent during a year when soda sales at large continued a many-year downward trend and 63 percent of consumers surveyed by the agency said that Fansville made them love Dr. Pepper more. The obvious question begged by these results, though, is, was it worth it? Was a 3 percent increase in sales worth the tens of millions spent by Dr. Pepper? And how much greater could that brand love have been if Dr. Pepper had simply made more college students' dreams come true?

Claire Embry is one of our social media analysts at Lippe Taylor. I was surprised to see that the Fansville Cannes Lion award entry from Deutsch LA (the advertising agency behind Fansville) claimed more than 300,000 people had commented about their advertising campaign on social media, so I asked her to look into it. Using NLP (natural-language processing) and AI, she was able to paint a much clearer and more believable picture of what actually happened.

TOTAL SOCIAL REACH

Source: Proprietary analytics using Brand Watch, Lippe Taylor Jan-Dec 2020.

Although there was a lot of conversation about Dr. Pepper during college football, the conversation about their scholarship program dwarfed that about their ad campaign. And with much more positive sentiment about the scholarship activation. The emojis being used in conversation also do a nice job of painting a picture of how consumers felt about these two marketing programs. Even though both programs received a lot of 🏈 emojis, the scholarship activation was acknowledged by 👏 🙌 📸 💰 , whereas conversations about the advertising campaign were accompanied by 😅 😵 💩 👻 ♀.

SOCIAL SENTIMENT BREAKDOWN

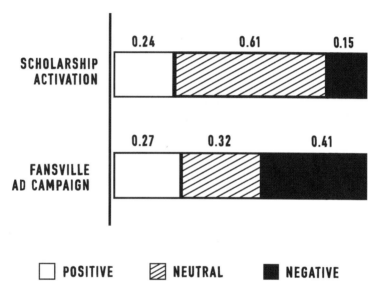

Source: Brandwatch.

Dr. Pepper's college tuition program is a great example of a top-drawer marketing activation, and Fansville is a great example of a top-drawer advertising campaign. However, no matter how much money is spent on the advertising, people still respond better to the activation.

Many advertising devotees will argue that marketing activations like the scholarship program *are* advertising. I disagree. "Activation" is a phrase that's become popular in recent years as a way of describing any number of marketing activities that are not traditional campaigns. I use it here to refer to things brands *do* as opposed to things they *say*. Think of Red Bull as an example; they run advertising campaigns that say "Red Bull gives you wings." This is just marketing-speak and it's an example of a brand saying something that has no real meaning. On the other hand, when it came time to launch the program behind Tom Schaar landing the first skateboarding 1080, Red Bull didn't just make an advertisement. They built a custom skate ramp and hosted an event for Tom to perform the stunt. This activation was then followed by an integrated PESO media plan that included having Tom himself interviewed by local news stations. This is a great example of a brand DOING something, not just advertising.

In fact, most of the best marketing campaigns of the last decade amount to being either purpose-driven or activation-centric. Think of the 180 videos whipped up by the Old Spice team in less than three days, engaging with people on social media. That was an activation that extended an advertising campaign. The activation is what everyone remembers, though. The same goes for Proactiv inviting consumers to paint a mural on a building in Brooklyn. Other famous examples include Coca-Cola's Share a Coke campaign where they printed people's names on their cans, State Street's Fearless Girl statue, Bud Light turning a ski town into the all-expenses-paid fanzone Whatever, USA, Mastercard's virtual fan wave for homebound soccer fans on TikTok, and the Taco Bell Hotel. These are all great examples of marketing activations that captured our attention because the brand was doing something, not just saying something.

COLLABORATE AS A STRATEGY

As media outlets have struggled to find revenue, many of them have begun to offer sponsored content opportunities. Groups like T Brand Studios at *The New York Times*, BrandVoice at *Forbes*, and *Newsweek* Amplify exemplify this. These media outlets are all doubling down on the claim that they, not Facebook, have the best understanding of how to influence their audiences.

The challenge for marketers is that working with half a dozen creative teams at media outlets is a lot less efficient than tasking your existing partner(s) with handling it. However, your existing partners likely have a limited worldview when it comes to how they work with media outlets. If they're a PR firm, they pitch for editorial coverage, and if they're an advertising agency (Creative or Media), they buy media inventory. Seb Tomich at *The New York Times* explains the future as one where brands will work with their agencies to develop a core concept, then collaborate with media outlets to tailor it for their audiences. This idea of collaborating with media outlets, rather than pitching them or buying inventory from them, is a surprisingly novel concept that offers great value for brands.

In one of the most inspirational examples of a brand embracing collaboration as a strategy, let's return to Intel. In the 1990s and 2000s, Intel managed to turn from B2B chip manufacturer into Intel Inside—the brand consumers demanded from laptop manufacturers. No doubt, advertising in those decades played an important role in this.

However, the company was struggling with the millennial generation who disdained advertising even in their teens and early twenties. This was the reason why @Intel was one of the first major companies to take social media seriously, and why Intel

CMO Deborah Conrad greenlit a massive collaboration with Vice Media many years before other companies had ever considered this kind of brand-media collaboration.

The Creators Project launched in 2010 as a $40 million partnership with Vice Media. In fact, Vice founder Shane Smith has publicly credited the campaign for turning Vice Media into the behemoth it became—telling *The Wall Street Journal* in 2016, "That program built the company. You learn, holy shit, we could do a $40 million deal with Intel where we actually create content that we like, and they don't give notes! Why were we doing banner ads?"

In reality, $40 million was a relatively small portion of Intel's marketing budget, but it was enough to procure a fully integrated collaboration where Intel would receive the best content Vice was capable of producing. Rather than Intel simply buying advertising space and running their own ads, the company funded Vice to create an ongoing content series about contemporary artists and how they created art with technology. The companies collaborated on the goals and the strategy, but Intel ceded content approval rights to Smith and his team at Vice, instead acknowledging that Vice knew best how to reach their millennial audience. The project ended up generating hundreds of millions of views and millions of engagements from the exact consumers Intel was trying to reach.

Source: The Treasury of Sanctuary in San Francisco as part of Intel's Creator Project 2012. Image credit: David Larkin

This may seem like a cherry-picked example given the scale of the budget and the relative cool factor of the Creators Project. However, examples abound where companies have engaged new audiences by creatively collaborating as a strategy. Consider, for example, the Leaps by Bayer program, which is a collaborative approach to developing new scientific breakthroughs and promoting them in partnership with *The New York Times*.

This collaboration started with Bayer's key message—that life-saving science is often met with resistance when first introduced. *The New York Times* content team then developed a three-part series that leveraged historical clips from their own newspaper to tell the story of how people had initially resisted important advancements such as the polio vaccine. It goes on to explain how Bayer is collaborating with would-be competitors such as CRISPR Therapeutics and Versant Ventures to create scientific leaps that are only possible by combining carefully guarded intellectual property from both companies. The ensuing scientific leaps—including gene editing for people with inherited diseases, development of stem cells to repair heart muscles after a heart attack, and genetically modified plants that can fertilize themselves—are expected to receive resistance among society. In addition to collaborating with external organizations to accelerate the science, Bayer is also collaborating with *The New York Times* to tell these stories in an audience-first way.

Ray Kerins is the SVP and Head of Corporate Affairs at Bayer Corp in the United States. He also chairs the Innovation Committee for the US Chamber of Commerce. Speaking about the Leaps by Bayer program, he explained to me, "The whole concept of *The New York Times* collaboration was for people to realize...before you go and shoot down science, first you have to understand the value to humanity. It's about changing the conversation." For Bayer to say that would have simply sounded defensive. By communicating the point in collaboration with *The New York Times*, who volunteered to quote their own historical archives, Bayer enlisted the kind of credentialing power of a third party that gets consumers on board. By surrendering control of the message to the content team at *The New York Times*, they demonstrated true collaboration and the resulting content comes across as being trustworthy.

Another successful example of a brand-media collaboration was the Proactiv #skinpositivity program described in Chapter 4. Rather than producing an anthemic campaign in our conference room and blasting it across the internet, we collaborated with the studio team at Teen Vogue. Together, we concepted and executed the program. Both Lippe Taylor and Teen Vogue were well compensated for the activation, but we did so as partners rather than as a media buyer and seller. In fact, collaborating with Teen Vogue as true partners was the defining aspect of the campaign's success.

Many DTC brands have experimented with advertising. However, in most instances, advertising played a minimal role in how these brands were built. In its place, "collabs" or collaborations played a major role. These DTC brands couldn't afford to compete with the paid media budgets of entrenched players; therefore, they got scrappy instead. Examples of this abound in the influencer marketing world, where DTC brands frequently launch "collab" product lines or kits that are designed and promoted in partnership with influencers.

The strategy extends beyond DTC brands and also beyond influencers, however.

Co-marketing campaigns have become some of the most discussed efforts in the marketing industry of late, with examples like Crocs partnering with KFC to launch slippers designed to look like fried chicken, Taco Bell launching Doritos-flavored taco shells, and BMW partnering with Louis Vuitton for luggage that fit perfectly into the trunk of their car.

Mikio Fujitsuka is currently the Head of Global Consumer Care and Marketing Value at Johnson & Johnson. In 2020, he was recognized as the Digital Marketing Leader of the Year by GDS Group. Several years ago, when Mikio was the brand manager on Band-Aid, he conducted a brand management masterclass for collaborating as a strategy. First, when it came time to launch the Quiltvent™ product for the Latinx community, Mikio went straight to Univision. Rather than producing the assets with his agency and then asking Univision to distribute them, Mikio collaborated with an all-Univision crew and gave them creative authority to produce the assets. He explained this to me as if it was so obvious, everybody should be doing it. "Univision's team knows much more about how to resonate with the US Hispanic audience because they're producing content for them every minute of the day," he said. In this case, Mikio prioritized what would resonate with the media company's audience over perfecting his commercial message. He also recognized his own team lacked proximity and familiarity with the audience, so he empowered the right people instead.

Mikio's commitment to collaborating as a strategy was not limited to unfamiliar audiences, though. Other examples include a Tongal partnership to launch blister bandages for foot care (Tongal crowdsources marketing videos from thousands of independent filmmakers who range from professionals to students) and becoming the very first external brand to be sold in J.Crew stores. At the time, J.Crew was one of the hottest brands with young consumers, and they had never sold any other brand in their stores. Simply asking them to sell Band-Aids was never going to work. Instead, Mikio explained his strategy to me by saying, "For me, it's all about affiliation branding. I want my brand to sit at the right lunch table. In order to get a seat at the cool table, you have to have equity with just one cool girl." J.Crew had the power to be that cool girl for Band-Aid. Following this strategy of building equity with a cooler brand, Mikio partnered with J.Crew's designers to design new denim-inspired Band-Aids, which were then featured in J.Crew catalogs and sold in J.Crew stores. Revenue from the partnership was enough to offset the costs of doing it, while the value from affiliation branding was enormous.

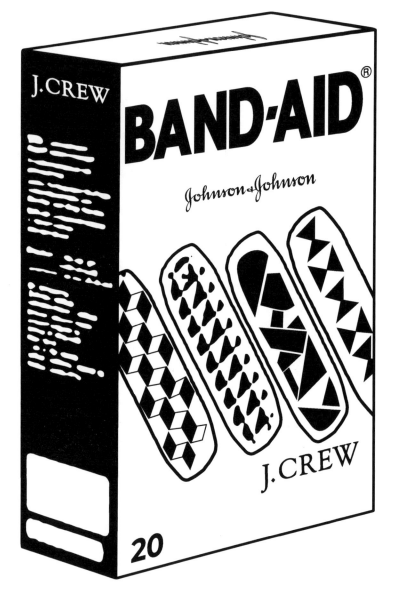

In addition to borrowing equity from other "cool" brands, the obvious appeal of collaborating as a strategy is that you can tap into the similar but adjacent audiences of the partner. Perhaps the less obvious value is that you learn more about your own audience based on how they engage with the partner and the campaign. These programs are usually resource-light in terms of paid media support but require time and effort to get right. Thankfully, social media analytics are a great resource here for identifying potential partners to collaborate with. Analyzing the following and content engagement behaviors of your own audience on social media means you can discover what other potential partners they are engaging with.

The easiest way to get started is to create a matrix of the potential types of partners you might collaborate with, interspersed with how you might collaborate. For example:

	MEDIA	INFLUENCERS	BRANDS	RETAILERS	NGO'S	ACADEMIA	DESTINATIONS
	(EG NYT, ABC, BUZZFEED)	(EG CELEBS, SOCIAL MEDIA STARS, PODCASTERS KOLS)	(EG NON-COMPETITIVE BRANDS YOUR CONSUMERS BUY)	(EG EXISTING SALES CHANNELS AND NON-SALES STORES AND WEBSITES)	(EG CHARITIES, DEVELOPMENT FUNDS THINK TANKS INTEREST GROUPS)	(EG SCHOOLS, RESEARCHERS, INSTITUTES)	(EG TOWNS, STADIUMS, MUSEUMS, LANDMARKS, PARKS)
PRODUCE CONTENT	X	X			X		X
REACH AUDIENCE	X	X	X	X			X
CREATE PRODUCTS		X	X	X			
CONDUCT RESEARCH	X				X	X	
HOST EXPERIENCE	X		X	X		X	X
ETC.							

Approaching these third parties with an aim to collaborate, armed with the insight that you have shared audiences, is a great place to start. The key to success is taking the term "collaboration" to heart. Rather than bringing a fully baked concept to the partner, it's important to start with a conversation about what you hope to achieve, and ask the same of them in return. Then you can collaborate together on a marketing plan that achieves both parties' objectives.

ENGAGE WITH YOUR AUDIENCES—DON'T TARGET THEM

The influence of Silicon Valley and its financiers has come to dominate a lot of mindshare in the marketing industry lately. Through a combination of AdTech and venture capital or private equity investors who demand hockey stick growth charts, technology, big data, and left-brain thinking have taken prominence over a traditionally creative industry. In order to achieve these kinds of valuations, companies have to create an aura of predictability about their performance, which is bolstered by claims that intellectual property, usually big data and software, will give them an edge and allow them to forecast their growth curve with a high degree of accuracy.

Two important trends are linked to this. The first is *performance marketing* in which brands only pay when a specific outcome is achieved—for instance, someone visits a website, signs up for more information, or makes a purchase. The second is *programmatic advertising*, which refers to software exchanges that use big data and AI to buy and sell advertising inventory almost like stocks. Brands can enter a budget, select a number of criteria about the consumers they want to target, and upload any number of different images and copy fragments. The software will then scour the exchanges in real time and place bids for available advertising slots, running an automated combination of your images and copy wherever it finds a cost-efficient place to put them.

On the surface, these philosophies make a lot of sense to ROI-obsessed marketers: why would I pay for something unless it generated results? And programmatic takes the risk out of media planning! I can just let the technology target consumers for me. Both of these marketing approaches have a role to play. However, Zenith now estimates more than 70 percent of digital advertising is bought and sold programmatically. As a result, its rise to prominence has affected the overall mood and way of thinking in the marketing industry.

This is perhaps most apparent in the explosion of what I call military marketing. Although military vernacular has always found a home in corporate conference rooms, the disruption of a traditionally creative industry by the bots of Silicon Valley has put the proverbial jet fuel on the trend. In fact, wartime lexicon has become so normalized that marketers don't think twice about *charging* their *lieutenants* with *targeting* and *acquiring* the people they want to sell products in a *mission-critical* type of *campaign*. Let's not forget the absurdity of referring to some of these efforts as the *tip of the spear.* Is it any wonder that, set against this backdrop, Big Advertising began to view consumers as adversaries who needed to be coerced and manipulated into capitulation? Even less nefarious creative briefs contain phrases such as *winning hearts and minds*, which itself is a construct born of the Vietnam War.

In fact, when looking at the *arsenal* or various *arrows in the quiver* of today's marketers, there are often partners *on board* for *boots on the ground* as well as *guerilla* and *surgical campaigns.* Somewhere within this craziness, the "hearts and minds" type of agencies, which typically hail from a public relations background, are most often asked to play second fiddle to an "agency of record," which hails from an advertising background. This agency of record invariably gives as much thought and prioritization to hearts and minds as the military does.

Despite being normalized by Silicon Valley, this kind of militaristic thinking has its roots in the zero-sum world of twentieth-century competition where brands fought one another for scarce and coveted shelf space in retail stores such as Walmart. In the modern economy, shelf space on the internet is literally endless. So what if instead of doing battle with our consumers, we engaged with them? What if instead of viewing them as targets to be acquired, we embraced them as partners in building the brand?

This is exactly how PR people think.

Despite the PR industry's many years in the wilderness, when the widespread failure of PR professionals to evolve with digital technology caused many marketers to view the profession as old school and narrow-minded, the earned media renaissance and accompanying decline in advertising effectiveness has brought PR firms surging back to the forefront. Meanwhile, their advertising counterparts are rapidly trying to develop "Earned Creative" capabilities.

In fact, this is exactly the reason I joined Lippe Taylor, an agency that has been known for decades as a leader in earned media. By the 2016 presidential election, almost all the major PR firms had rebranded themselves to drop the "PR" nomenclature. Their once-large media relations teams had shrunk, sometimes so marginalized that they hired freelancers for it. And yet, in 2016, every other post I saw on social media was a news article...with no PR firms left, plus a totally saturated advertising and digital marketing landscape, the decisions by Facebook and Google to offer algorithmic priority to news content meant that earned media had paradoxically become the rare and valuable piece in the marketing mix.

There is no doubt that earned media has its limitations. Despite Bill Gates's famous quote that if he had only one dollar left, he would spend it on public relations, the truth is that editorial inventory is scarce and procuring positive ink for your brand is difficult and unpredictable.

As millennials have become the defining generation of consumer behavior, there is a clear trend toward marketing programs that are worth talking about. These programs are almost always ideas that were born from an "Earned Creative" way of thinking. Earned Creative is an industry-wide concept that was popularized by Edelman, the largest PR firm in the world. It refers to marketing concepts that are inherently engaging—meaning they invite engagement from journalists and consumers alike.

Advertising agencies are also embracing this trend. In fact, although for many years the trend was PR firms trying to become more like ad agencies, the opposite is now also true.

Advertising agencies are now trying to become more like PR firms. These agencies are embracing terms such as "agility" and "being nimble" while featuring their Earned Creative chops in their showcase reels where TV commercials once dominated. The type of frictionless marketing described in this book is not public relations or advertising. It is a hybrid form of marketing that some agencies are embracing more than others.

Regardless of the type of agency you work with, the key is to think through the lens of engaging your audiences rather than targeting them. You should of course still use analytics and precision in the pursuit of efficiency and ROI. However, the mental framing through which you view the marketing program should be first through the lens of *what will people engage with?* Catherine Hernandez-Blades appears frequently on lists of the most influential marketing and communications leaders. One of her great innovations is what she calls the 4Es. As part of our Lippe Taylor speaker series, Catherine explained, "Today, you have to provide an **environment** with **experiences** that people will **engage** with while creating opportunities for **exchange**." This book has provided a lot of tools for how to do this: listening and responding to consumers, contributing to societal conversations, building a brand through partner affiliation, prioritizing activations over advertising, leveraging social proof, and more. However, none of these tools will work unless you shift your mental model away from targeting consumers and think instead about engaging with them.

In my experience, the programs that best achieve this ideal of being inherently engaging are concepted from an Earned mentality first and foremost. This is where ideas originate that are naturally interesting to the advertising-averse generation. These ideas—those that will spark coverage and conversation—are also much more nuanced, timely, and difficult to pull off. This is exactly why you should plan with an Earned philosophy first, then turn your attention to paid media after you've landed on a great Earned Creative concept.

We're going to talk in the next section about scaling your marketing efforts through paid media, and programmatic can absolutely be a part of this. However, because of the relative speed with which left-brain thinking and military marketing has swarmed the industry, and the executive-level appeal of removing the human error and relying on ROI-tuning machines for marketing, it's important that the overarching guidance for your marketing strategy is one of engaging consumers rather than targeting them. Leave the targeting to the bots and prioritize an engaging marketing philosophy first and foremost.

SCALE IT AS THE LAST THING YOU DO

In most large companies, paid media is one of the largest line items in the marketing budget. As I said in the Introduction, despite my passion for marketing without advertising, I'm also a realist. Advertising as we know it may be dead, but paid media is still an important component in the marketing mix. The problem isn't that brands use paid media; it's that they allow paid media to dominate or lead their marketing strategy. Paid media is best used to bring scale to an otherwise smart and engaging marketing activation. However, because it represents such a large budget line, the temptation for most marketers is to plan Paid first. This is the mistake most commonly made in large, entrenched brands because they have the luxury of large paid media budgets.

The challenger brands competing with them don't have these budgets. Somewhat counterintuitively, this becomes the challenger brand's greatest asset because they're forced to think of marketing ideas that are actually interesting to people. As a result, the disruption they deliver often looks an awful lot like the LACES framework.

For marketers at market-leading or entrenched heritage brands, it is possible to turn this advantage on its head. However, you have to do three things that are entirely countercultural. In fact, you will likely encounter all five of the fundamental dilemmas in your attempts to do so. These are:

1. Pretend you don't have a paid media budget until the very end of the planning process.
2. Reserve dry powder to use opportunistically.
3. Rip up the measurement methodology for your media buying agency.

Plan Paid Last

Start by pretending you don't have a paid media budget. Sounds simple enough, right? Of course, your media agency will present endless reasons why it's a bad idea (you'll miss out on the best deals, all the premium advertising spots will be gone, media consumption insights should integrate with creative, etc.). Your sales forecasting tools are heavily reliant on inputting paid media support, and your CFO isn't going to accept *trust me, I'm going to be nimble and agile all year long* as the business rationale for your budget.

But if you can pull it off, designing a marketing plan without paid media support, then planning the paid media last, gives you a very good chance of coming up with something that people will engage with.

Challenge your creative teams—what would we do with zero budget for paid media? This will force you to plan with an Activation, Collaboration, and Engagement-first mentality, rather than the Paid-first mentality that delivers advertising campaigns to audiences that are outright saying to you, *I don't want to be advertised to.* Once you have the ideas set, then you can scale them with paid media.

No matter how much budget is set aside for paid media, if you think of it like a scale tactic rather than a leading strategy, you will wind up creating marketing plans that are inherently interesting. Then, once you've completed the rest of the marketing plan, you can put your paid media budget back on the table and consider how you would spend it. In most cases, you will be scaling and amplifying a great idea instead of placing an advertisement. Finally, always remember to keep some dry powder.

The Case for Saving Dry Powder

The stranglehold that large media companies held over market-ing budgets through up-fronts (large, up-front commitments made by brands to buy blocks of advertising) is largely on its way out. However, because of the role paid media plays in sales fore-casting, most brands still allocate nearly all of their paid media budget early in the year. Although there are internal reasons for doing this, it also deprives you of the opportunity to take advan-tage of relevant cultural moments in a bigger way. In fact, most challenger brands exist on a monthly budgeting cycle rather than annual. The amount of paid media they have to spend in February is literally dependent on how many new customers they got in January. It's no wonder they seem to be more agile and able to quickly jump on trending topics. I recommend withholding at least 20 percent of your paid media budget to use opportunis-tically throughout the year on things such as media moments, cultural events, and partnership opportunities.

Measure Media Differently

Most media buying agencies are measured on media-specific metrics. It's reasoned that because they don't control the cre-ative, they can't be entirely responsible for whether the marketing works. However, they can be held responsible for whether the media reaches a certain number of targeted people and how much it costs. Therefore, your media agency is always working to optimize a simple ROI formula: reaching as many targeted people as possible, while spending as little money as possible. Sounds smart, right?

In practice, however, what happens is that the media agency refuses to support creative ideas that don't fit in their existing framework. This is especially true once an annual plan has been set and yearly KPIs agreed upon. They become a forcing mechanism for stagnation. So while Sebastian at *The New York Times* is innovating new ways of partnering with brands, your media agency has no incentive to collaborate with him until a best practice comes along that fits his new advertising approach into the ROI formula of their annual plan. In other words, you will literally never be an innovator.

What if instead you followed Andy England's example from Coors Light and measured the media buying agency based on how well they support your activations? What if you segmented off paid support for collaborating as a strategy, recognizing it would not fit in the existing ROI formula? And of course, what if you reserved a sizable portion of your paid media budget to use opportunistically throughout the year? You would not be able to measure the traditional KPIs in the same way. However, you would be scaling marketing programs that today's consumer wants to engage with.

RETHINKING YOUR WHO

In this book, I have put forth my best effort to explain WHY marketers need to make wholesale changes to their marketing programs, and for most of this chapter I have endeavored to provide a framework for HOW they can accomplish this. However, as with most significant changes, moving to a frictionless marketing philosophy requires more than simply rethinking the why and the how of your marketing efforts. It also requires reframing the WHO in more ways than one. Specifically, whom you collaborate with and whom you define as your customer. Let's take these in reverse order.

WHO IS YOUR CUSTOMER?

Along with the age-old question, *what business are we in?*, one of the marketing thought experiments that has spawned the greatest opportunity for consultants in recent years is the question, *who is my customer?* Until the 2010s, this was a typically straightforward question. It was the people who bought whatever you were selling. If you were Coca-Cola, that meant Walmart. If you were a medical device manufacturer, it meant surgeons. If you were a hardware company, that meant ITDMs (information technology decision makers). If you were the CEO of a publicly traded company, that meant the investors who bought your stock. And so on. This simplistic view of who the customer was has changed dramatically in the last ten years, though.

Much like marketing and media have been consumerized, there are very few industries that have remained untouched by consumerization. Even industries that traditionally dismissed consumers as unimportant have been upended. The best examples are industries where consumers are typically labeled as something else—something less important than the primary customers. Examples of this include higher education, technology, insurance, and pharmaceuticals. In higher education, consumers are labeled as *students*, while technology companies refer to them as *users*, insurance companies call them *members*, and pharmaceutical companies call them *patients*. In all four of these cases, the manufacturer or service provider is distanced from the consumer and works through some sort of third party (often an authority figure) to deliver its offering.

These are also all examples of industries that have recently been disrupted by consumerization. Higher education is perhaps the most approachable of these examples. A quick Google search reveals two common trends in higher education today: colleges and universities competing in the amenities arms race (trendy dining options, lazy rivers, indoor beaches) and college professors complaining about how entitled students today expect to receive A grades regardless of their effort or ability.

The latter of these trends is supported empirically by a boom in peer-reviewed articles by scholars examining everything from the root cause of student entitlement to its negative effects on the college learning environment. All this is set against a backdrop of runaway costs that has captured national attention. In fact, although the average cost of college has increased nearly fivefold since 1990, the number of scholarly articles mentioning "entitlement" and "college students" has increased twentyfold.

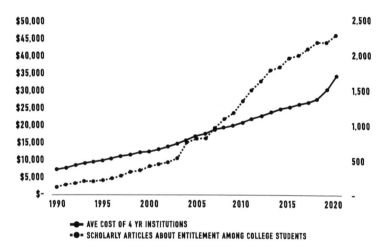

AVE COST OF 4 YR INSTITUTIONS
SCHOLARLY ARTICLES ABOUT ENTITLEMENT AMONG COLLEGE STUDENTS

Source: National Center for Education Statistics and Google Scholar 2021.

Is it any wonder, when consumers shift from paying relatively little to relatively a lot for their education, that they now expect good grades? The power dynamic that protected institutions of higher education was one of authority—professors were in charge, students had to comply or face expulsion. That dynamic is totally different when a student becomes a customer, and at $40,000 per year, everyone is a customer.

The same dynamic is happening with pharmaceuticals. Where doctors were once clearly defined as the customer, that's rapidly changing. From 2008 to 2017, the average deductible for patients with employer-sponsored health insurance rose from $869 to $1,808. Average real costs paid by patients per year have likewise doubled, meaning patients are rapidly becoming customers. Doctors who refuse to write prescriptions report the same kind of response from entitled patients with a Google diagnosis as professors report from C students. No matter what business you are in, the eventual cost paid by consumers for your offering is directly related to how much influence they exert over your corporate ecosystem. If that cost is going up, you should expect consumers to be a more important stakeholder in the future. Not only was this inevitable to a degree, as consumers become accustomed to being the customer in everything they do, it will only accelerate their expectations of every company they interact with. B2B companies, public utilities, and even government organizations need to come to terms with the consumer being their customer. Because with consumerization comes inevitable expectations and disruption—disintermediation of middlemen (including retailers), loss of pricing power, and preference for challenger brands, disruption by digital-native competitors, and so forth. It also brings new demands for the kind of consumer-first marketing programs described in this book.

WHOM YOU PARTNER WITH

Despite a significant trend toward in-sourcing recently, marketing service providers will always be an important part of the ecosystem for brand marketers. In particular, advertising, public relations, digital marketing, and media buying agencies have developed the core competencies to be strategic partners while a long list of specialized players—production houses, talent agencies, promotions and shopper marketing agencies, and many more—have developed niche offerings that offer a lot of value.

I've had an opportunity to work very closely with the largest and most awarded agencies in most of these disciplines. I've also interviewed thousands and hired hundreds of people from all agency backgrounds. As a student of our industry, I always take time to ask questions and learn more about how each of these different agencies is run. What they're good at, what their weaknesses are, and what I can learn from the people who lead them. There are no doubt very smart people in every kind of agency and successful marketing programs are born from every corner of the industry. There is also a lot to be said for the role that chemistry, trust, and partnership play in a brand's marketing success. As the Silicon Valley saying goes, always get behind an A-team with a B-idea rather than a B-team with an A-idea.

However, all things being equal, there are marked differences between how different types of agencies operate and the work they produce. Traditional ad agencies are built to make ads. Their ideas rarely work unless you promote them with ads. Traditional PR firms are built to pitch media. Their ideas rarely scale beyond today's news cycle. Traditional digital agencies are built to drive web traffic. Their ideas rarely engage people off-line. And so on.

Note that I'm referring here to the "traditional" notions of each agency type, when of course many agencies are investing in redefining and modernizing themselves as we speak. It's also worth noting that agencies exist simply to merchandise people's time and ideas. They can always surprise you with great ideas even outside the bounds of what the agency exists to create.

As an example of this, many of the amazing marketing programs described in this book were created by advertising agencies. However, the ideas I featured were inherently "Earned" ideas— meaning they were worth talking about on their own, even if there had been no advertising to promote them. Although advertising agencies are full of smart people, they are not designed to generate this kind of thinking. In fact, Earned Creative ideas represent a tiny portion of the work being produced by advertising agencies overall, and the internal processes at these agencies make it less likely, rather than more likely, that these kinds of ideas will make it to the client. It would be a mistake to believe these outlier examples mean advertising agencies are well suited to doing this kind of work.

When I interview creative director candidates from Big Advertising agencies in particular, this is a purposeful part of the interview process. I have to answer the question, "Do they understand what constitutes an idea versus a concept?" "Concepting" is advertising parlance for thinking up ideas. However, the output of concepting can oftentimes be more like a set of words than an actual idea. For example, we hired a creative director for a test project to promote the luxury chocolate brand GODIVA. He came back with the idea of, *Taste the Luxe Life*. "Nice," I said. "What is it?" He spent the next ten minutes explaining why GODIVA should be associated with living a luxurious life, which frankly seemed obvious to everyone. "That concept only works if we make an ad about," I told him.

The problem is that he didn't understand the difference between a concept and an idea. His **concept** could create the impression that GODIVA is part of a luxurious lifestyle...but only if we made ads about. An **idea**, on the other hand, would have been something like, partner with Tiffany jewelers to create GODIVA chocolate earrings, thus conveying the impression of GODIVA being part of a luxury lifestyle. This would be an example of the brand doing something worth talking about.

This distinction illustrates not only the difference between activations versus advertisements but also why advertising agencies are ill-suited to lead your marketing strategy in this new era. Certainly, plenty of ad agencies have come up with good activation ideas over the years. However, they are structured first and foremost to concept advertisements. And the vast majority of their work reflects it.

I'm really proud of the creative team we've built at Lippe Taylor, under the leadership of industry veteran Tina Cervera. Tina has led creative teams at Big Advertising agencies, owned her own consultancy, and made a name for herself by building the 350-person, social media-first creative team at Vayner Media, all before coming to Lippe Taylor as our Chief Creative Officer. She understands the difference between a concept and an idea and breeds that thinking in the team.

An example of a recent marketing activation that illustrates this point was when Tom Hanks was cast in the lead role for the upcoming Mr. Rogers film, *A Beautiful Day in the Neighborhood*. Ancestry.com was Lippe Taylor's client and we worked with their researchers to discover that Tom Hanks was in fact related to Mr. Rogers (they were sixth cousins). We were reasonably sure that nobody knew of the connection, including Tom himself. Therefore, our media rock star Keri Madonna worked with *Access Hollywood* to surprise Tom and his wife with the news (along with the late Fred Rogers's widow) on the red carpet premiere of the film with an Ancestry-provided family tree.

The revelation was surprising and timely enough that people started including mentions of Ancestry every time they talked about the film, sparking a viral sensation touching nearly every major media outlet and millions of social media conversations. In fact, more than 500 million earned media impressions accompanied the campaign and almost half of all social media conversation about the film mentioned Ancestry. The idea behind this activation—to reveal a celebrity's surprising and culturally relevant family history, could very well have been made into an ad campaign. Even Tom Hanks himself could have been cast to promote how important family history is. That would be an advertising concept, though, and it wouldn't be worth talking about.

There is no doubt that good ideas can come from anywhere. However, the structure and talent pool of PR firms and social media agencies are undoubtedly best suited to concepting activation ideas. These are the agencies where people have always thought through the lens of "what will get people talking?" without the benefit of being able to force them into consuming an advertisement. It's also why I chose to ply my trade in a PR firm when many of the top ad agencies were recruiting me. Activations are the heart of great marketing for today's consumer, and PR firms are the best partners to design your activations. Advertising agencies have a role to play when it comes time to create ads about your marketing program.

CONCLUSION

Michael Bloomberg made his fortune selling both premium content subscriptions via the Bloomberg Terminal and advertising via Bloomberg News. And when it came time for his biggest investment ever, he turned to advertising to carry the day. Much like every political contest of our lifetimes, the prevailing wisdom was that whoever spent the most on advertising was destined to win.

Bloomberg's catastrophic failure heralded the end of an era. It was the end of the era where anybody could *buy* their way to success if they spent enough money on advertising. It turns out that consumers are savvier than we gave them credit for and that after decades of being tormented by advertising, they've decided that the constant friction in their lives simply isn't worth it.[52]

---

52   Nick Corasaniti and Lazaro Gamio, "The Extraordinary Scale of Bloomberg's Ads, in 6 Charts," *The New York Times*, February 26, 2020, https://www.nytimes.com/interactive/2020/02/26/us/politics/michael-bloomberg-ad-campaign-spending.html.

The demise of advertising will not be quick nor will it be complete. Big Advertising as it was is over. Yet, brands still need to market themselves, and media companies can't make enough money selling content. There will be a reduced role for advertising in the media landscape. But there will also be a gap that remains—a gap between brands that need to meet marketing goals and the available channels for doing so. How are you going to fill that gap for your brand?

FORTUNE FAVORS THE BOLD

After several hours in a balloon ascent to an altitude of 120,000 feet on October 14, 2012, a man stepped out onto the platform of a now-hovering spacecraft and dived back to the earth's surface. On his way, he captured the attention of eight million people (sixteen times the Olympics at its peak), nearly breaking YouTube while he himself broke the sound barrier, traveling 833 mph and becoming the first human to go supersonic without being in a jet or spacecraft. That man was Felix Baumgartner, and without Red Bull, his extraordinary stunt would never have happened. For twenty-three seconds, mid-freefall, Felix spun dangerously out of control while panicked producers switched away to a live feed of the empty launch pod for fear he would lose consciousness and plummet to his death. Red Bull is known for risk taking. Thinking back to Tom Schaar's attempts to land a 1080 half a year earlier, that stunt could have failed. But with Felix, the risks were of a different magnitude. In the end, the saga that had started seven years prior, providing a drumbeat of intrigue and publicity for Red Bull throughout, ended with Felix Baumgartner landing safely in the Arizona desert.

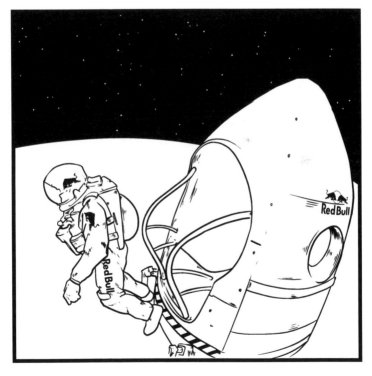

Source: Felix Baumgartner, October 15, 2012. Red Bull Content Pool.

The Red Bull Stratos activation was one of the most dramatic and risky marketing stunts ever attempted, but it was undertaken with a clear strategic intent. For Baumgartner himself, his goal was to inspire a younger generation the same way men landing on the moon had inspired him. For Red Bull, it was also about inspiring that same generation, because no matter how it had ended for Felix Baumgartner, it was Red Bull that had given him wings.

Werner Brell was the President of Red Bull Media House at the time of Stratos. He said to me shortly after that he believed breaking new ground was in the DNA of the company; however, he hoped to see lots of brands following in the trail Red Bull was blazing.

In the book *Leap: How to Thrive in a World Where Everything Can Be Copied*, Howard Yu writes, "Seizing a window of opportunity, which means not necessarily being the first mover but the first to get it right, takes courage and determination. To leap successfully is to master these two seemingly contradictory abilities. The discipline to wait and the determination to drive, in balanced combination, often pay off handsomely."[53] Not every brand needs to blaze trails like Red Bull. In fact, most brands should wait to seize the window of opportunity at the right moment.

Whether with SEO, social media, analytics, influencer marketing, or the return of earned media, I've had a knack for embracing transformative trends at the right time—once the trend has taken hold but before widespread adoption turns a competitive opportunity into table stakes. The time is now to listen to consumers and give them the kind of marketing they've been asking

---

53   Howard Yu, *Leap: How to Thrive in a World Where Everything Can Be Copied* (New York: PublicAffairs, 2018).

for. Advertising needs to take a back seat, and marketers should focus on providing people with a frictionless brand experience.

In the same book, Yu also asserts that "thinking doesn't equate to doing," reminding us that simply recognizing these trends and agreeing something must change isn't sufficient. It takes leadership to leap. CeraVe's example is illustrative in this regard.

AN OVERNIGHT SUCCESS...AFTER YEARS OF INVESTMENT

In January 2020, Tom Allison, co-founder of CeraVe, approached twenty-four-year-old Hyram Yarbro, known on TikTok as @ skincarebyhyram, who had previously voiced his support for the brand. Allison was offering Hyram an official brand ambassador partnership.[54] Hyram's videos are entertaining and educational, and although he doesn't claim to be a licensed professional in any way, his product reviews and skincare routines are highly influential. With his seven million TikTok followers and more than four million YouTube subscribers, his approach was resonating with Gen Z in particular.

In the first half of 2020, CeraVe posted double-digit growth in all zones contributing to a 29 percent increase in operating profits for L'Oréal's Active Cosmetics Division. All this during a period where L'Oréal's like-for-like sales were down almost 12 percent. CeraVe itself was credited with a 100 percent month-over-month sales increase during the month of June, with @skincarebyhyram pinpointed by multiple industry analysts as the sole impetus behind the meteoric growth.

54   Jennifer Weil, "TikTok Turned This Brand into a Cult Favorite," WWD, December 7, 2020, https://wwd.com/beauty-industry-news/beauty-features/watch-story-behind-cerave-success-hyram-tiktok-1234668920/.

The reaction across the skincare industry was like a sonic boom. Executives at Procter & Gamble, Johnson & Johnson, Kao Corporation, and Galderma all rushed to figure out how CeraVe had seemingly captured lightning in a bottle with a single influencer on TikTok.

L'Oréal's Chairman and Chief Executive Jean-Paul Agon, after sharing that CeraVe was up 82 percent through the first nine months of 2020 and had sold out in some markets, said on a call in October that the success resulted from "the right quality, the right formula with the right mix at the right moment."[55] By year end, the brand had done $600 million in sales.

Competitors like Johnson & Johnson launched countermarketing initiatives aimed entirely at "blunting" the growth of CeraVe. The brand was viewed as public enemy number one in the skincare aisle, but largely its success was also downplayed as a totally unforeseeable stroke of luck.

In truth, CeraVe's activity in social media and with influencers had been a staple in the brand's marketing plan for years. It may be tempting to believe they stepped up to the plate and hit a home run on the first swing, but the brand had countless at-bats beforehand. Hyram is just one of 2,300 influencers (+134 percent from 2019, 1,700 influencers) who created about 9,000 pieces of content for CeraVe in 2020, a 183 percent increase from the year prior when they created about 4,900. Fortune favors the bold but also the committed. While their competitors were still running "test and learns" or dipping a proverbial toe in the water, CeraVe had made a meaningful and ongoing commitment, which was the foundation of their success.

---

55   Jennifer Weil, "How CeraVe Ruled the Internet," Yahoo!Life, December 5, 2020, https://www.yahoo.com/lifestyle/cerave-ruled-internet-050153744.html.

In a proprietary analytics study conducted by Lippe Taylor using data from YouGov and our internal Hypatia Gravity Score®, we found that during the same time period, Johnson & Johnson had the most effective advertisements in skincare. In fact, Ad Awareness for their brands was not only very high, but it also correlated strongly with Purchase Consideration. For CeraVe, Ad Awareness was not nearly as high. However, Earned Media Impact and WOM Exposure (people who claim to have heard about the brand via word-of-mouth) were extremely high for CeraVe. And not only did they correlate with Purchase Consideration but with Purchase Intent as well.

CeraVe is now one of the most relevant brands among the Gen Z audience. While their competitors were optimizing and tweaking advertising-led playbooks, CeraVe leaped.

DISRUPT YOURSELF

In *The Innovator's Dilemma*, the late Clayton Christensen describes how entrenched market leaders—in part because of their position and in part because of the management practices that allow them to maintain such an advantage—have little short-run incentive to explore the small or thin-margin opportunities presented by even potentially disruptive technologies.

Unfortunately, given the five fundamental dilemmas, many brand marketers find themselves in a similar situation. They know advertising doesn't work like it used to. They see the writing on the wall when it comes to the popularity of premium content subscriptions and anti-advertising sentiment. But they also have a job to do right here, right now. And when you consider what's worked in the past, it's a safer bet to make small tweaks rather than wholesale leaps.

One of the healthiest ways of breaking free of this funk is to imagine you were a new market entrant that was trying to disrupt your own brand. What would you do? What would you not do?

Seb Tomich describes a prescient conversation he had with a senior executive of *The New York Times*. As Global Head of Advertising, Seb was grappling with a familiar dilemma. The company was making tens of millions of dollars by selling programmatic ad inventory on open market exchanges. These ads were typically low quality, poorly designed, and most definitely not specific to the *Times*'s audience. He told the executive the ads went against an audience-obsessed philosophy, but they were generating a lot of revenue for the company. This executive told him to flip the problem around and view it from a different perspective. "Imagine we didn't have a programmatic ad business at all," he said, "and someone came to us and offered us tens of millions of dollars to put these low-quality ads on our apps. Would you do it?" Seb admits the decision was then perfectly clear. They canceled the programmatic ad business in 2019 as they continued their pursuit of being an audience-obsessed advertising business.

Brand marketers can apply the same kind of thinking to their own advertising plans. It's not to say that very many marketers have the freedom to forgo tens of millions of revenue in pursuit of a greater vision or that entrenched leaders should necessarily do the same things that challenger brands do. But if you believe Eisenhower's famous assertion that plans are useless while the act of planning is invaluable, then it would be a worthwhile effort to try writing your marketing plan without advertising at all. Look at it through the lens of, *If I was the disruptor brand myself, what would I do?*

Netflix provides a quintessential example of disrupting their brand—and their industry. Their move from mail-order DVDs to streaming is a well-documented case study. In 2012, CEO Reed Hastings predicted the decline of DVDs and decided to burn the proverbial ships by going all in on streaming. "We expect DVD subscribers to decline steadily, every quarter, forever," he said on an earnings call that year.

By 2019, their DVD rental business did about $300 million, a tiny fraction of their more than $20 billion in total revenues. Many thought that by giving up on mail-order DVDs and investing so much in streaming that the company was going to go under. In fact, their stock price tanked after Hasting's announcement. However, in 2020, it was sitting well above $500 per share.

A similarly well-known example is Steve Jobs's decision at Apple to cut numerous product lines to focus on a mere handful. That led to the iPod, the iPhone, and the iPad. When there are fewer products, they have to succeed, and the people working on them have nowhere to hide. Accountability goes through the roof in that environment.

I'm not suggesting that every brand needs to immediately burn the ships as ruthlessly as Hastings, Jobs, or *The New York Times*. But if you want to market your brand in a way that resonates with today's consumer, it will require moving from a "test and learn" approach to a "this has to work" mentality. That means putting your traditionally effective tactics such as advertising on the back burner while you put real focus and resources into the LACES framework.

Brand marketers can be the ones to set a vision for how marketing evolves at their companies, bringing trends, ideas, and new approaches forward to senior leadership. They might have to start by disrupting their own brand first, though.

STAY IN THE GAME

I mentor a lot of young professionals who inevitably wind up asking the question "Should I go back to school?" at some point. It's usually in relation to seeking an MBA or sometimes a master's degree. Alternatively, they wonder if a lesser focus on education—maybe a few online courses—would be beneficial. In most cases, they can see a future vision for themselves, but they're not sure how to get there from their current position. Therefore, they wonder if they need to totally disrupt the path they're on in order to ultimately achieve that future vision. Invariably, my advice to them is the same: your career will be better off if you stay in the game instead of going back to an MBA or master's program. By the same token, taking a handful of online courses that don't culminate in a larger outcome (e.g., a degree) is often a waste of time. This doesn't necessarily mean eschewing education, but it does mean committing to a larger program with night or weekend classes so you can stay in the game at work while pursuing a larger outcome at school.

The same advice applies to embracing a frictionless marketing philosophy. If you can see the future vision, that's half the battle. The other half is charting a course from where you are today. I don't actually recommend totally disrupting the path you're on and starting over. However, just adding in some test-and-learns won't amount to a larger outcome either. Brands that commonly follow this approach find themselves with underperforming social media, influencer marketing, and experiential components to their marketing plan because they took the "online course" approach. They underinvested in "tests," not knowing what to expect, and then pulled out when the tactics underwhelmed. The problem is, today's consumer likes engaging with brands that are committed to the same channels and topics that they are. And nailing the brand voice for these channels requires a lot of practice.

Success at the scale of Hyram for CeraVe requires significant and sustained investment. Home runs like Oreo's Dunk in the Dark require consistently showing up. Oreo had executed what it called the Daily Twist—that is, a daily post about something happening in culture, for a hundred days before the Super Bowl. Success requires commitment. It's not a short-lived test, and it's not entirely self-serving. Brands that devote all of their social media budget to buying ads never break through with consumers. Today's consumer expects brands to invest in building goodwill on the channels. And like your career progression, successfully evolving your marketing approach requires staying in the game today while committing to a future outcome. Test-and-learns aren't going to cut it.

No doubt, the return on this kind of investment is not as predictable as data-driven marketers would like. CeraVe produced 9,000 pieces of content with influencers in 2020. In order to do that, the brand had to let go and empower their partners. Each piece of content wasn't scrutinized for the right calls to action, and measurement was reserved for the whole body of work, rather than trying to attribute value to every piece of the puzzle. It's a great example, though, of how staying in the game leads to a brand becoming better and better at the craft, while gaining more and more respect from consumers.

In the simplest terms, being bold may mean making a commitment to being where your consumers are and engaging them in ways they want to be engaged. The entrenched ecosystem of marketing measurement will not reward you with clear and obvious KPIs right away. However, if you stay in the game, you will be rewarded by your consumers once they realize you're a serious player.

DON'T WASTE THIS CRISIS

When talking about the desperation-induced home run that was Old Spice's *The Man Your Man Could Smell Like*, Michael Sabbia harkens back to the timeless idiom to "Never waste a crisis." In truth, many brands today are in a more precarious position.

True crises of the sort faced by Old Spice act as a galvanizing force, rallying teams together and leading to the obvious decision that disruptive thinking is the only way forward.

For most brands today, there is no great crisis thrusting them into chaos. Instead, there is the slow and methodical degradation of underlying and difficult-to-measure things such as cultural relevance, consumer perception, and brand value. In many ways, it's similar to a cancer that spreads undetected rather than a sudden health event that inspires you to take action.

So the question is, will brand marketers treat cancer detection and treatment with the seriousness that it deserves? Or will they continue to tweak their current diet and hope for the best? The collapse of advertising and wholesale changes represented by the consumerization of media is a crisis for brand marketers. And like all crises, it represents an opportunity for those who treat it as such.

THE ANSWER LIES IN YOUR OWN BEHAVIOR

When you go to Google, are you searching for a "cheap" product or the "best" product? Whom do you trust when it comes to picking the "best" product? When you log in to Spotify, are you listening to the ads? What do you do when a television commercial comes on? The truth is easier to see once you grapple with your own cognitive dissonance. If you're searching for "best" product recommendations and then marketing a brand by blasting commercial messages with little endorsement from third parties, then it's time to take note. If you're spending $10 million a year on advertising and then skipping the ads in your personal life, the time is now to disrupt your own plans. The effects of 2020 have led to terrible uncertainty. However, the obvious trend toward less advertising was blown wide open.

Although it may be tempting to believe the collapse of advertising was caused by the events of 2020, the pandemic only accelerated the trends. Advertising effectiveness had already plummeted, and it was the result of a systemic failure in the advertising model. For those brand marketers who see this, the question now is, what to do about it? To what degree will advertising continue to deliver enough value to earn another year of prominence in your marketing plan? To what degree will consumers continue to avoid, block, or eliminate your marketing messages?

Marketing has been consumerized. Media companies are adapting. Consumers want a different kind of marketing. But brand marketers face fundamental dilemmas when trying to adapt to this new expectation of frictionless marketing. This book provided a way of thinking and a framework for how you can adapt.

The frictionless marketing movement is here. Brand marketers who examine their own prioritizations and change their beliefs about advertising can be on the front of that wave. Big Advertising will remain alluring. But the type of marketing consumers expect is now apparent, and the time is now to leap to a different strategy.

How you leap is up to you.